Class 2

ENGLISH GRAMMAR & COMPOSITION

Concepts & Practice

WORKBOOK

DISHA™
Publication Inc

DISHA Publications Inc.

A-23 FIEE Complex, Okhla Phase II
New Delhi-110020
Tel: 49842349/ 49842350

Typeset By
DISHA DTP Team

Buying books from DISHA

Just Got A Lot More Rewarding!!!

We at DISHA Publication, value your feedback immensely and to show our apperciation of our reviewers, we have launched a review contest.

To participate in this reward scheme, just follow these quick and simple steps:
- Write a review of the product you purchase on Amazon/Flipkart.
- Take a screenshot/photo of your review.
- Mail it to **disha-rewards@aiets.co.in**, along with all your details.

Each month, selected reviewers will win exciting gifts from
DISHA Publication. Note that the rewards for each month
will be declared in the first week of next month on our website.

https://bit.ly/review-reward-disha.

Write To
Us At

feedback_disha@aiets.co.in

CONTENTS

Sentences

A sentence is a group of words that gives a complete meaning.

> **Please note:**
> - **A sentence tells us a complete thought.**
>
> **For example:**
>
> **Incorrect:** He is (Does not tells us what is "he" doing)
>
> **Correct:** He is eating. (Tells us what "he" is doing)
>
> - **A sentence can have any number of words.**
>
> **For example:**
>
> (a)   I am tall.   (b)   He will go to school.

SUBJECT & PREDICATE

A sentence can be broken into two parts: subject and predicate

Subject:

- *Subject is usually the first part of a sentence.*
- *A subject is either a noun (person, place, thing, or animal), a noun phrase.* (*My dog, her doll, their house*) *or a pronoun* (*he, she, it, I, we, they, his, her, their, your*).

For example:

(a)   **Pingu** is a penguin. (**Pingu** is the name of a bird. So it is a noun. Here Pingu is the **subject**.)

(b)   **He** is very naughty. (**He** is a pronoun. So he is the **subject** here.)

Predicate:

- *A predicate is a group of words in a sentence without the subject.*
- *It tells us something about the subject.*
- *A predicate will have a verb or action word in it.*

For example:

(a) Tina is **watching television.** (Here **'watching television'** is the **predicate**. It tells us something about the subject 'Tina'.)

(b) He **looks good.** (Here **'looks good'** is the **predicate**. It tells us something about the subject **'He'.**)

TYPES OF SENTENCES

There are two types of sentences:

1. Declarative Sentences

A declarative sentence makes a statement. It states a fact or truth. It always ends with a period (.)

For example:

(a) This is my book.

(b) Reema is going home tomorrow.

This is a dress.

2. Interrogative Sentences

An interrogative sentence asks a question. It always ends with a question mark (?)

For example:

(a) Is this my book?

(b) Are we going out?

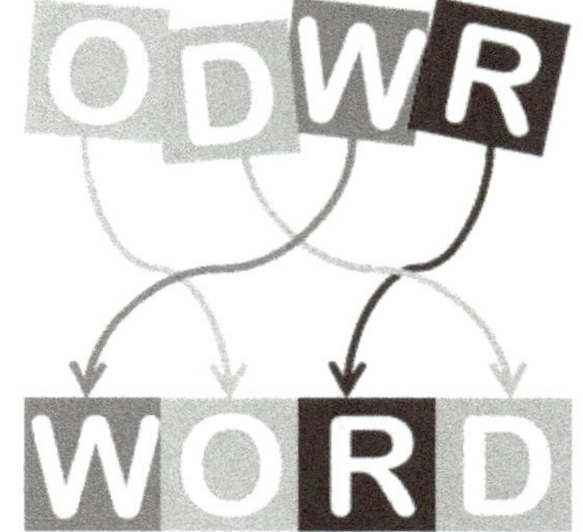

Is it raining?

JUMBLED WORDS AND SENTENCES

goln	opst
unr	olev

These words don't make any sense because the letters are not in the correct order or they are scrambled. Now, let's unscramble them and make meaningful words.

Long	Stop
Run	Love

Similarly, sentences will not make sense if the words are not in the correct order or scrambled.

Let's see a few examples of scrambled sentences.

go I school to	eat? we can now
play with me? you will	live in India I

Now let's unscramble them.

I go to school.	Can we eat now?
Will you play with me?	I live in India.

Name : _______________________

Section : _____________

Assessment Technique:

Application Based Worksheet

Home Work

Marks : 20

Time : 1 Day

I. **Directions: Separate the subject and predicate of the following sentences.**

$(1 \times 10 = 10 \text{ marks})$

1. I want a new car.
   Subject: _____________________
   Predicate: _____________________

2. Rajiv is nice.
   Subject: _____________________
   Predicate: _____________________

3. The sun is moving.
   Subject: _____________________
   Predicate: _____________________

4. Kavita wrote the letter.
   Subject: _____________________
   Predicate: _____________________

5. The letter was written by Namita.
   Subject: _____________________
   Predicate: _____________________

6. The farmers are ploughing the field.
   Subject: _____________________
   Predicate: _____________________

7. Sachin Tendulkar is an amazing player.
   Subject: _____________________
   Predicate: _____________________

8. The storm clouds are getting darker.
   Subject: _____________________
   Predicate: _____________________

9. Dogs, cats and rabbits make the best pets.
   Subject: _____________________
   Predicate: _____________________

10. All people of the town ran away from the burning building.
    Subject: _____________________
    Predicate: _____________________

II. Directions: Choose a predicate to complete each sentence given below.

(1 × 5 = 5 marks)

> cut the boy's hair, watered the flowers, blew in the wind, barked all night long, flew the air plane.

1. The gardener ____.

2. The pilot ____.

3. The little puppy ____.

4. The barber ____.

5. The flag ____.

III. Directions: Choose a subject to complete each sentence. (1 × 5 = 5 marks)

> A grey dolphin, A buzzing bee, A big spider, The house plant, An eye doctor.

1. _______ looked for nectar in the flower.

2. _______ checked my vision.

3. _______ needs soil, water and sunlight.

4. _______ jumped in the sea.

5. _______ spun a web in the doorway.

Name : _______________________

Section : _____________

Assessment Technique:

Fillers

I. Directions: Identify if the given sentences are declarative or interrogative sentences. Write 'D' in blank if sentence is declarative and 'I' if sentence is interrogative.

(½ × 10 = 5 marks)

1. I play with my dog.   ___________
2. Do you know Radha?   ___________
3. I am a student.   ___________
4. Are you eight years old?   ___________
5. Gopal is hungry.   ___________
6. They are clowns.   ___________
7. Where is my diary?   ___________
8. Do you have a pet dog?   ___________
9. She is my little sister.   ___________
10. The old man was a kind man.   ___________

II. Directions: Some answers are given below. Supply questions using suitable question words. One has been done for you. (Use separate sheet.)   (½ × 10 = 5 marks)

1. Tejas's birthday party is on 19th June.

   <u>When is Tejas's birthday party ?</u>

2. The little baby is fine now.

3. Yes, I am taking my medicines.

4. My mother gave me these chocolates.

5. My grandmother lives in Delhi city.

6. Aviral won the all rounder award this year.

7. I like to play chess and scrabble.

8. I like the red ball.

9. I could not come to your birthday party as I was not well.

10. I fell from the stairs.

Name : ______________________________

Section : _______________

Assessment Technique:

Jumble Fumble

Class Work

Marks : 20

Time : 30 Minutes

Directions: Arrange the jumbled words given below to make meaningful sentences.

(2 × 10 = 20 marks)

1. today / happy / I / feeling / very / am

   ____

2. flying / birds / the / sky / in / are

   ____

3. good / Radhika / student / a / is

   ____

4. Sreeram / sister / fighting / always / is / with / his

   ____

5. watching / T.V / health / to / injurious / is / time / a / long / for

   ____

6. love / children / food / to / fast / eat

   ____

7. pray / least / once / every / at / day / must/we

   ____

8. have / house / I / a / dog / my / in

   ____

9. must / exercise / we / daily

   ____

10. is / a / broken / lobby / there / chair / in / the

    ____

Name : _______________________________

Section : _____________

Assessment Technique:

Jumble Fumble

Home Work

Marks : 20

Time : 1 Day

I. Directions: Re-arrange the jumbled words to make meaningful sentences.

$(1 \times 10 = 10 \text{ marks})$

1. the in stars shine sky _______________________________________

2. us cow milk gives _______________________________________

3. have brother I elder an _______________________________________

4. sister naughty my very is _______________________________________

5. fly sky kites the in _______________________________________

6. trees are on hill the there _______________________________________

7. should we trees protect _______________________________________

8. gardener plants the waters _______________________________________

9. go where you do to want _______________________________________

10. like do book you this _______________________________________

II. Directions: Unscramble the given words.

$(1 \times 10 = 10 \text{ marks})$

1. efink _______________

2. eyrt _______________

3. kcol _______________

4. incha _______________

5. neov _______________

6. theig _______________

7. esroh _______________

8. batsel _______________

9. bronwia _______________

10. soume _______________

CHAPTER 2

Synonyms, Homonyms and Homophones

SYNONYMS

When two or more words have similar meaning, they are known as synonyms.

For example:

Big – huge – Large

All three words mean big. So they are synonyms of each other.

Why do we use synonyms?

- It makes our writing and reading skills better.
- It helps us in not repeating the same word again and again.
- It increases our vocabulary.

Usage of Synonyms:

Let's use the word beautiful as an example. The synonyms of beautiful are:

Beautiful – pretty – good looking

Now let's use these synonyms in sentences.

(a) Shruti is **beautiful.**   (b) Shruti is **pretty.**   (c) Shruti is **good looking.**

List of Common Synonyms:

Word	Synonym
Big	Large
High	Tall
Little	Small
Nice	Kind
Mad	Angry
Quick	Fast

HOMONYMS

A homonym is a word which is spelled and pronounced the same way as another word but their meanings are different.

For example: Can

(a)   Can I help you? (Here **can** is used to take permission).

(b)   Please open this can of coke. (Here **can** means a tin can which keeps food and liquid.)

Example:

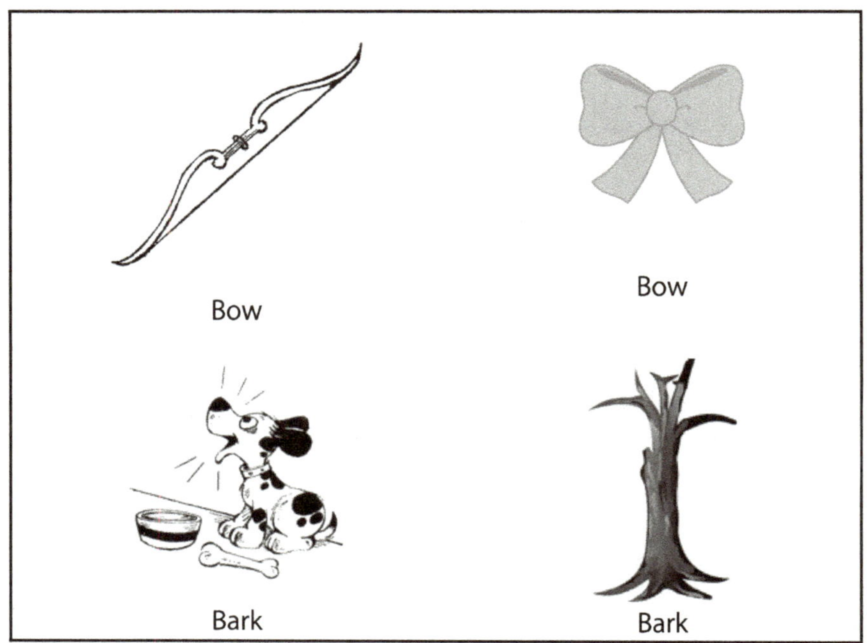

List of Homonyms

Homonym	Meaning
Bear	1. A big furry animal 2. To tolerate
Left	1. To leave behind 2. A direction
May	1. Month of May 2. To show something is possible
Ring	1. A metal band to wear on one's fingers 2. To call someone
Hide	1. An animal's skin 2. To keep a secret

A homophone is a word which is pronounced the same way as another word but their meanings and spellings are different.

For example: Knew and New

(a)   This dress is new. (New means introduced recently)

(b)   I knew you won't come to school. (Knew means knowing something)

For example:

| Ate | Eight |
| Week | Weak |

List of Homophones

Homophone	Meaning
Watch	To look or see
Watch	A thing which tells us the time and is worn on the wrist
Two	The number 2
Too	Also
Ate	Past tense of eat
Eight	The number 8
Be	To exist
Bee	An insect
Beat	To hurt someone
Beet	A vegetable
Break	To smash
Brake	To stop

Name : _______________________

Section : _____________

Assessment Technique:

MCQ Based Worksheet

I.   Directions : Mark the correct synonym of the words given below: (½ × 8 = 4 marks)

1.   Build

(a) carry ☐   (b) make ☐   (c) change ☐

2.   Brave

(a) smart ☐   (b) good ☐   (c) fearless ☐

3.   Grow

(a) develop ☐   (b) begin ☐   (c) construct ☐

4.   Decide

(a) cut ☐   (b) make ☐   (c) fix ☐

5.   Cunning

(a) helpful ☐   (b) clever ☐   (c) wise ☐

6.   Fade

(a) bright ☐   (b) colourful ☐   (c) dim ☐

7.   Junk

(a) rubbish ☐   (b) good ☐   (c) fall ☐

8.   Holy

(a) good ☐   (b) godly ☐   (c) pure ☐

II. Directions: Rewrite the sentences replacing the underlined words with words from the box.   **(1 × 6 = 6 marks)**

1. Suresh always keeps his bedroom <u>tidy</u>.

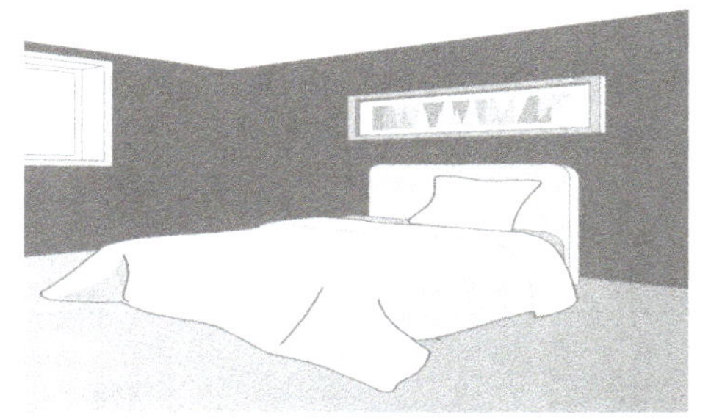

____

____

2. The monkey <u>jumped</u> off the tree trunk.

____

____

3. Mahesh likes to live in a <u>big</u> house.

____

____

4. The landlord <u>yelled</u> at the boys for plucking the mangoes.

____

____

5. Everyone started laughing when the <u>clown</u> walked in.

____

____

6. Rupa is a <u>lovely</u> girl.

____

____

Name : ___________________________	Assessment Technique:
Section : _______________	**Fill-ins**

Class Work

Marks : 10   Time : 30 Minutes

I. **Directions: Given below are six words which have to be used in the given sentences. Each word is to be used twice. Read the sentences carefully and select the words that fit properly in the sentence.** (½ × 10 = 5 marks)

free,	table,	cross,	ruler,	left,	break

1. We should ____________________ the road carefully.

2. Shivaji was a great ____________________.

3. I was ____________________ alone in the park.

4. We had popcorn and Pepsi during the movie ____________________.

5. When I opened my pencil box, the ____________________ was missing.

6. Take a ____________________ turn for the school.

7. 'Rohan! Hold the glass carefully otherwise it will ____________________', said Sarita.

8. The teacher asked the students to ____________________ the wrong answer.

9. Please come! Dinner is served on the dinning ____________________.

10. He got an eraser ____________________ on purchase of a box of pencils.

II. **Directions : Read the passage given below and fill in the blanks with a correct word from the options given below.** (5 marks)

Yesterday I saw a __(1)__. It wanted me to free it from a cage. __(2)__ was too scared of doing so. So I came without looking at it. __(3)__ passed, I did not go via that place. It was __(4)__ tough to avoid going there. But I would turn __(5)__ instead of going straight where that animal was kept in the cage. We should not keep animals in cages. We all love our freedom. Animals must also be loving it.

1. (a) hare   (b) hair   (c) here   (d) hear

2. (a) eye   (b) I   (c) Ei   (d) Ii

3. (a) Daze   (b) Days   (c) Dais   (d) Dazes

4. (a) vary   (b) very   (c) berry   (d) veri

5. (a) right   (b) write   (c) rite   (d) wright

CHAPTER 3

Naming Words

What if someone says, **"Bring me the thing on which we sit."**

Or

"Bring me the thing which is used to write."

Or

"We went to a place nearby a river."

Did you understand what thing is the person asking for?

We can sit on many things – **chair, sofa, stool, bed.**

We can use different things to write – **pen, pencil, crayon, coloured pens.**

We can visit any place, near any river – **Calcutta, Kerala, London, Paris.**

A naming word names a person, place, thing or animal. Naming words are also called **Nouns.**

For example:

Chair, Cow, Man, Ruchi, India, Delhi

In order to talk to each other more clearly we need to know the names of people, things, place, and animals. Naming words helps us in doing that.

TYPES OF NAMING WORDS

1. **Common Nouns**

    Common nouns are names given to general items. It is a **name given to anything**, **any place**, **any person** or **any animal**. We see common nouns everywhere we go.

    For example:

    A bed, a chair, a cupboard, a table – these are common nouns.

2. **Proper Nouns**

    Proper nouns are names given to specific items. They are **names of people, names of books, names of places, names of rivers, names of mountains** and **names of buildings.** They always begin with a capital letter, even if they occur in the middle of a sentence.

    For example:

    Mahatma Gandhi, Yamuna river, Ramesh, Pluto, India – these are proper nouns.

Let's learn the difference between common nouns and proper nouns through examples.

(a)   The **book** that I read is very interesting. (Common noun)

(b)   **Jungle Book** is very interesting. (Proper noun)

(c)   **Puppies** are cute. (Common noun)

(d)   My puppy, **Fluffy,** is cute. (Proper noun)

COMMON NOUNS

Common nouns you will find in your bedroom.

| Chair | Bed and Pillows | Cupboard | Lamp | Table |

Common nouns you can find in your living room.

| Cushion | Flowerpot | Sofa | Television | Painting |

Common nouns you can find in your kitchen.

| Stove | Plate | Knife | Refrigerator | Glass | Cup |

Common nouns you can find in your bathroom.

| Comb | Toothbrush | Mirror | Soap |

Common nouns you can find in a classroom.

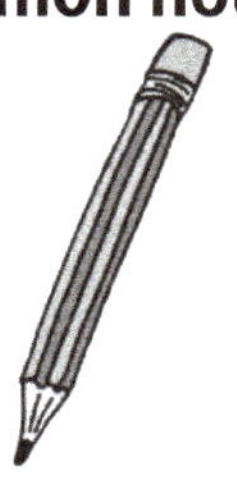
Pencil

Blackboard, Chalk, Duster

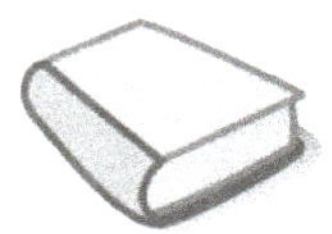
Book

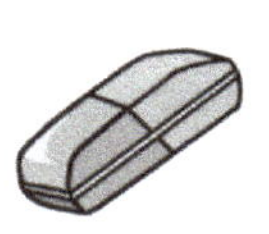
Eraser

Bag

PROPER NOUNS

Names of people

Mahatma Gandhi

Mother Teresa

Sachin Tendulkar

Sania Mirza

Names of places

Mumbai	Delhi	Chandigarh	Kerala
Kolkata	Goa	Jaipur	London
Paris	Tokyo	Germany	India
China	America	Connaught Place	Lajpat Nagar
	Gujarat	Chowpatty	Juhu

Names of rivers

Nile

Ganges

Yamuna

Yellow River

Congo

Hooghly

Names of books

Harry Potter, The Cat in the Hat, Roald Dahl Matilda, Famous Five

Names of mountains

Mount Everest, Himalayas, Shivalik

Names of Festivals

- **Religious Festivals**

Festivals that are celebrated by one religious group are known as religious festivals. In India, people of different religions live together – Hindus, Muslims, Sikhs, and Christians. Therefore Indians celebrate many festivals. Some of them are as follows:

Holi

- Holi is a festival of colours celebrated mostly by Hindus in North India.
- On this day, people play with colours and water.
- It is a day when family and friends meet. We wish each other on Holi by saying **"Happy Holi"**.

Eid ul Fitr

- Eid ul- fitr or Id is celebrated by Muslims all over the world.
- They fast from sunrise to sunset for one month before Eid.
- On the day of Id, they offer prayers to God.
- It is celebrated among family and friends by eating good food, exchanging gifts known as eidis. One gets to eat delicious dishes such as Biryanis, Kebabs and Sewaiyan. We wish each other on Eid by saying **"Eid Mubarak"**.

Durga Puja

- Durga Puja is celebrated in the month of September or October. It is celebrated on a grand level in West Bengal. It is a festival of ten days.
- During this time, Goddess Durga is worshipped.
- This festival is celebrated because Goddess Durga killed the dangerous Rakhshasha Mahisasur. We wish each other on Durga Puja by saying "**Happy Durga Puja**".

Diwali

- Diwali is known as the festival of lights.
- It is celebrated because Lord Rama returned home to Ayodhya after spending 14 years away. Diwali is celebrated mostly by Hindus.
- On this day, people decorate their homes with candles and lights and worship Lord Ganesha and Goddess Lakshmi. They exchange gifts and sweets among family and friends.
- People also burst crackers. But one should remember that bursting crackers is not good for our surroundings. We wish each other on Diwali by saying "**Happy Diwali**".

Christmas

- Christmas is celebrated on 25th December all over the world. It is mostly celebrated by Christians. Christmas is celebrated because it is the birthday of Jesus Christ. On this day, people decorate their houses. They put up Christmas trees and decorate it too.
- All the family members come together and exchange gifts. We wish each other on Christmas by saying "**Merry Christmas**".

- **National Festivals**

Festivals that are celebrated by the whole nation are known as national festivals.
They are:

Republic Day

India became a republic on **26th January, 1950**. It means that India's constitution (set of rules) was forced on this day. We celebrate it as **Republic Day**.

Republic Day is a national holiday. The main function is held at Rajpath in New Delhi.

The Republic Day Parade is very famous. People from different parts of the country walk in this parade, representing the place they belong to.

For example: Kashimiris from Kashmir, Biharis form Bihar, Punjabis from Punjab.

Independence Day

India became independent on **15th August, 1947.** So **Independence Day** is celebrated on 15th August every year.

On this day, the Prime Minister of our country raises the flag of our country at the Red Fort and gives a speech.

People hoist our national flag all over the country. Independence Day is a national holiday.

Gandhi Jayanti

We celebrate **Gandhi Jayanti** because it is the **birthday of Mahatma Gandhi**.

Mohan Das Karamchand Gandhi (Mahatma Gandhi) is the Father of our nation. He made our country independent from the British rule.

Therefore we celebrate his birthday, **2nd October**, as Gandhi Jayanti.

Gandhi Jayanti is a national holiday.

1. **Swings:** A seat hanging by ropes, on which one sits and moves back and forth.
2. **Slide:** A smooth slope on which children slide.
3. **Tire swing:** A swing made of a car's tire.
4. **Seesaw:** A long, flat piece of wood that is balanced in the middle so that when one end goes up the other end goes down.
5. **Sandbox:** A box containing sand where children play.
6. **Bench**: A long wooden seat where several people can sit.
7. **Bicycle:** A vehicle that has two wheels and a pedal. It moves when you push the pedal with your feet.
8. **Kite:** A toy made of paper which can fly in the air.
9. **Tree**: A woody, tall plant which has branches and leaves.
10. **Grass**: Long narrow leaves that grow on the ground.

Bicycle

Bench

Grass

Trees

Slide

Sandbox

Seesaw

Kite

Tire Swing

Swing

3. **Countable Nouns**

People, places, things or animals that can be counted are known as countable nouns. Countable nouns can also take the plural form.

For example:

Countable noun	**Plural**	**Countable noun**	**Plural**
Book	Books	Boy	Boys
Girl	Girls	Table	Tables
Glass	Glasses	Dog	Dogs

One orange	Two oranges	One Book	Four books

Uncountable Noun

Anything that cannot be counted is known as an uncountable noun. Uncountable nouns always take the singular form. They do not form plural form.

For example:

Water – Correct **Waters** – Incorrect	**Bread** – Correct **Breads** – Incorrect	**Rice** – Correct **Rices** – Incorrect	**Milk** – Correct **Milks** – Incorrect
Butter – Correct **Butters** – Incorrect	**Air** - Correct **Airs** – Incorrect	**Chalk** - Correct **Chalks** – Incorrect	**Food** - Correct **Foods** – Incorrect

Name : _______________________________

Assessment Technique:

Picture Based

Section : _______________

Class Work

Marks : 10

Time : 25 Minutes

I. Directions: State the type of noun displayed in the pictures given below.

(1 × 5 = 5 marks)

1. Geetika ....Noun Abhishek

2. Grandmother ....Noun Grandfather

3. Rubber ....Noun Pencil

4. Mickey mouse ....Noun Pluto

5. Mount Everest ....Noun Map of India

II. Directions: Look at the following pictures. Classify them into Proper and Common Nouns. Mark P for Proper and C for Common Noun in the box provided.

(½ × 10 = 5 marks)

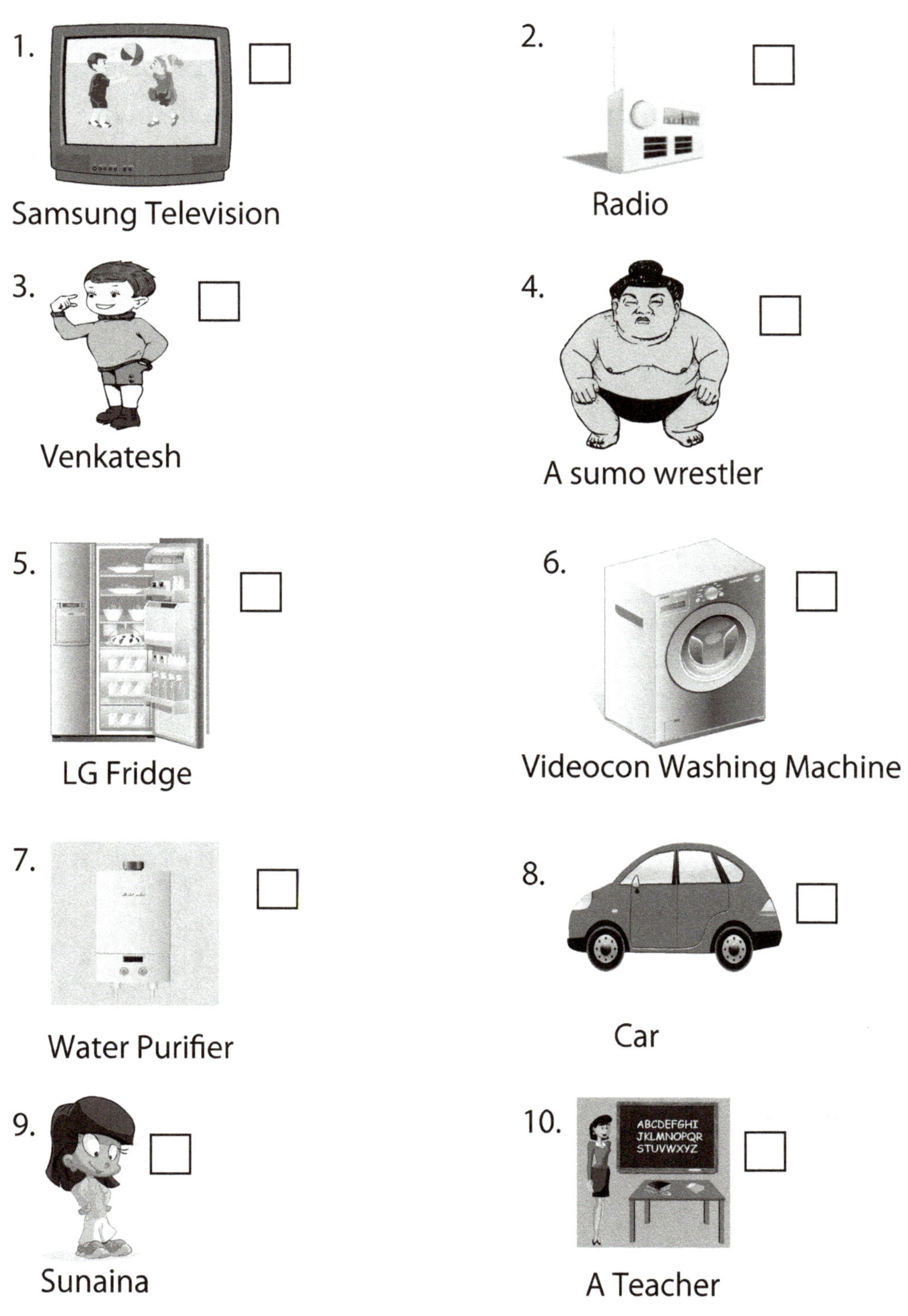

Name : _______________________

Section : _____________

Assessment Technique:

Picture Based

Marks : 10   Time : 1 Day

I.   Directions: Look at the images, write 'C' for countable nouns and 'U' for uncountable nouns.

(½ × 10 = 5 marks)

| 1. __________ | 2. __________ | 3. __________ | 4. __________ | 5. __________ |
| 6. __________ | 7. __________ | 8. __________ | 9. __________ | 10. __________ |

II. Directions: Classify the words in the box as countable or uncountable nouns.

(½ × 10 = 5 marks)

ketchup, cat, clock, pineapple, rice, honey, onions, tea, pens, flour

Countable Nouns	Uncountable Nouns

Name : ___________________________

Section : _____________

Assessment Technique:

Picture Based

Marks : 10

Time : 35 Minutes

I.   Directions: Identify and unscramble the words to get correct name of the national festivals. (1 × 3 = 3 marks)

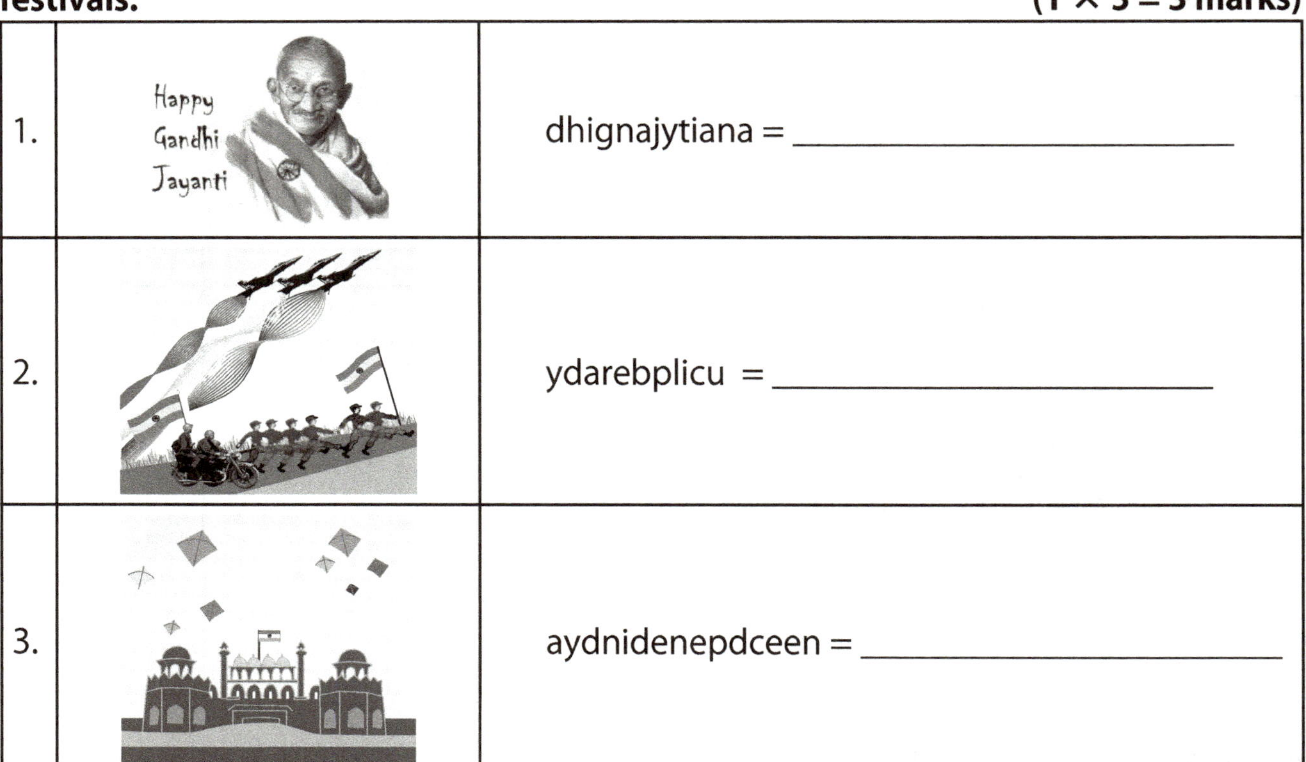

1.		dhignajytiana = ___________________________
2.		ydarebplicu = ___________________________
3.		aydnidenepdceen = ___________________________

II.   Directions: Identify clues and write the names of festivals. (1 × 7 = 7 marks)

1.   Festivals of lights   -   ___________________________

2.   Festivals of colours   -   ___________________________

3.   Festival when Santa give gifts to children   -   ___________________________

4.   Festival of victory of Good over Evil   -   ___________________________

5.   Harvest festival of Punjab   -   ___________________________

6.   Festival when sisters tie rakhi on brother's wrist   - ___________________________

7.   Birthday of Lord Krishna   -   ___________________________

Name : ___________________________

Assessment Technique:

Picture Based

Section : _______________

Class Work

Marks : 10

Time : 20 Minutes

I. **Directions: Write the names of the things you see in the park. You can make use of clue box.**

(1 × 5 = 5 marks)

slide   swing   round about   see-saw   frame

1. 

____

2. 

____

3. 

____

4. 

____

5. 

____

II. **Directions: Look at the picture below and write five sentences about it. (Use separate sheet.) One example has been done for you**

(1 × 5 = 5 marks)

Roopa went to the park. She saw ____.

CHAPTER 4

Accessories

An item of clothing or a piece of jewellery that one wears to add to one's basic outfit is known as an accessory. Men and women use and wear different accessories most of the time.

For example:

Jewellery, gloves, scarves, etc.

The names of some accessories for men and women may remain the same. But they look very different.

For example:

A man's hat does not have flowers attached to it, whereas a woman's hat has flowers and other decorations attached to it.

List of Accessories for Men/Boys

1. **Cap:** A soft, flat covering worn on the head.

2. **Belt:** A strip of leather or cloth worn around the waist hold trousers and pants.

3. **Socks:** A garment for the foot which keeps the feet warm.

4. **Shoes:** A hard covering for the foot which protect the foot from getting dirty.

5. **Gloves:** A woolen garment worn on both the hands to keep them warm.

6. **Sweater:** A woolen garment worn on the upper part of the body.

7. **Coat:** A long, woolen garment worn on the upper part of the body.

8. **Wallet:** A small folding object used for keeping money.

9. **Tie:** A strip of fabric material worn around the neck on formal occasions.

10. **Hat:** A round shaped covering for the head used to keep the head warm.

List of Accessories Worn by Women/Girls

1. **Earrings:** A piece of jewellery for the ears.

2. **Bracelet:** A piece of jewellery worn on the wrists.

3. **Necklace:** A piece of jewellery worn around the neck.

4. **Scarf:** A piece of cloth, like silk or cotton, wrapped around the neck.

5. **Ring:** A metal band worn on the fingers.

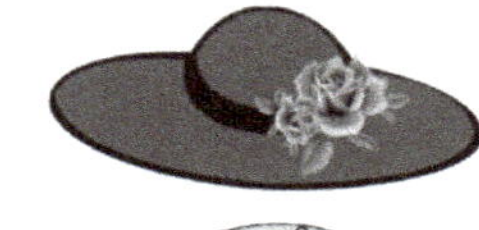

6. **Shoes:** A hard covering that protects the foot. For example, sandals, heels.

7. **Hat:** A decorative covering for the head used to keep the head warm.

8. **Cardigan:** A woolen garment worn on the upper part of the body by women.

9. **Alice bands:** Hair bands which are used to keep the hair away from one's face.

10. **Purse:** A small bag used by women to keep money.

Name : ______________________________

Section : _______________

Assessment Technique:

Picture Based

Home Work

Marks : **10**   Time : **1 Day**

Directions : Reena and Mehul have shifted to a new house. Their clothes and accessories are all mixed up. Help them to arrange their clothes and accessories in their wardrobe. Write the name of the clothes and accessories in the space provided.(½ × 20 =10 marks)

Wardrobe of Mehul		Wardrobe of Reena
1. _______________		1. _______________
2. _______________		2. _______________
3. _______________		3. _______________
4. _______________		4. _______________
5. _______________		5. _______________
6. _______________		6. _______________
7. _______________		7. _______________
8. _______________		8. _______________
9. _______________		9. _______________
10. ______________		10. ______________

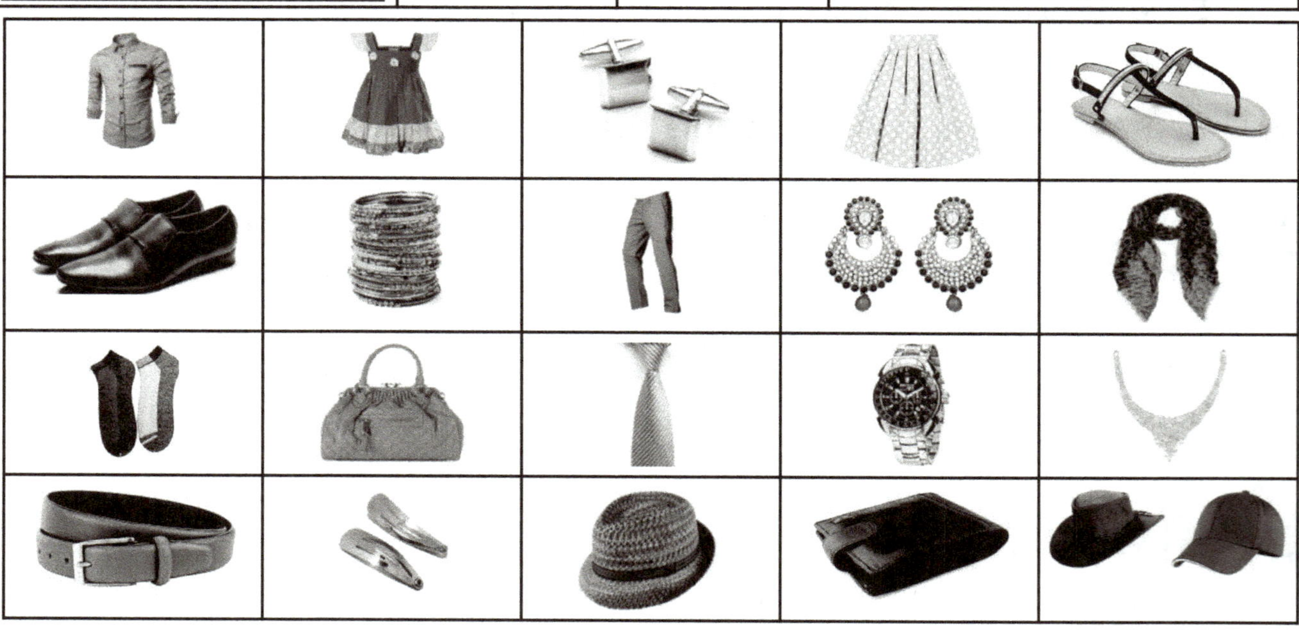

Food

Food, Glorious Food

Food is a very important part of our life. Food gives us energy to perform actions.

Let's learn more about different types of food.

Food Items:

1. **Fruits**: A sweet or sour product of a plant or a tree which can be eaten without cooking.

| Banana | Grapes | Mango | Orange | Apple |

2. **Vegetables:** A part of plant which is eaten as food. It is mostly eaten after cooking.

| Brinjal | Cucumber | Spinach | Onion | Potato |

3. **Dairy:** Any food product which is made from milk.

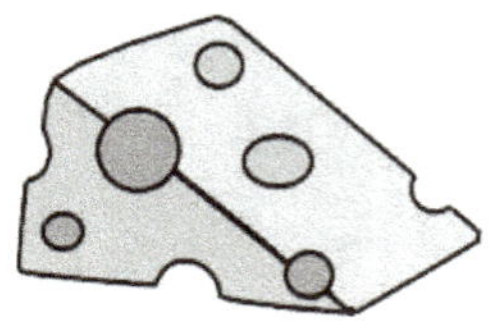

Cheese

Cream

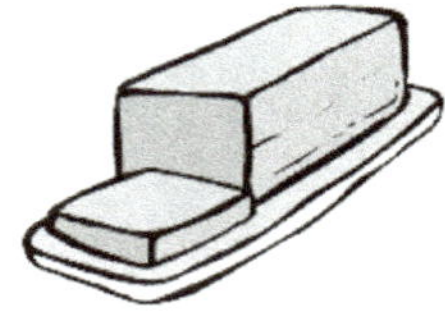

Butter

4. **Meat:** The flesh of an animal that is eaten as food.

Chicken

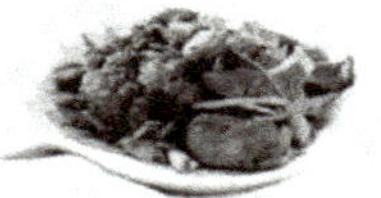

Mutton (meat from Goat)

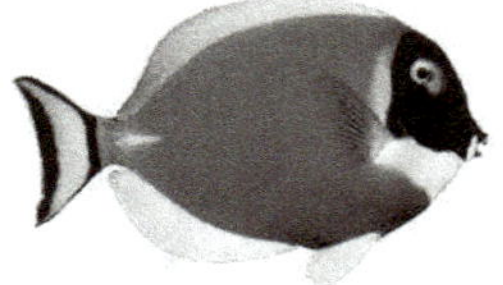

Fish

5. **Grains:** A part of a crop plant, such as wheat, rice, etc. It is eaten after cooking it.

Oats

Rice

Wheat

6. **Egg:** An oval object with a hard shell around it. We eat eggs given by hens. Eggs are mostly eaten after cooking.

Eggs

7. **Dish**: When we cook different food items, it is known as a dish.
   (a) **Burger** – A dish made with bread, meat, cheese and vegetables
   (b) **Pizza** – A dish made with bread, vegetables, cheese, sauce and meat pieces
   (c) **Bread** – A baked food made of flour and water
   (d) **Chappatis** – An Indian bread made with wheat flour
   (e) **Curry** – Vegetables or meat cooked with oil and spices
   (f) **Sunny side up** – A dish made from eggs
   (g) **Sandwich** – A dish made by putting vegetables or meat or cheese between two slices of bread.
   (h) **Soup** – A liquid dish made by boiling vegetables, fish, or meat.

Curry

Soup

Chappati

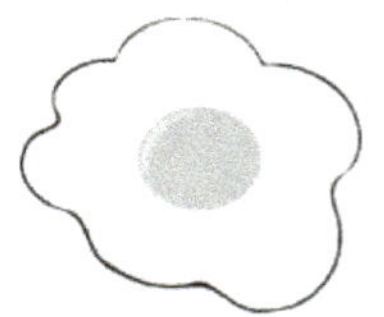

Sunny Side up

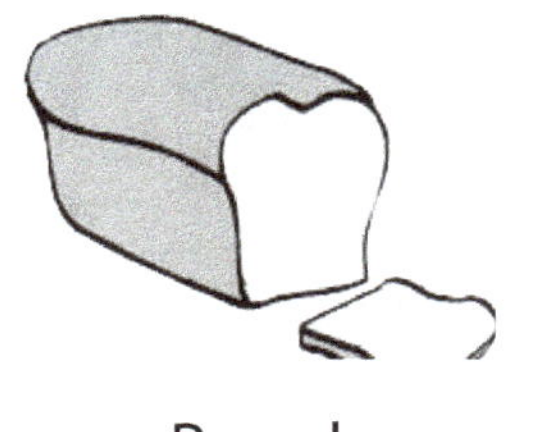

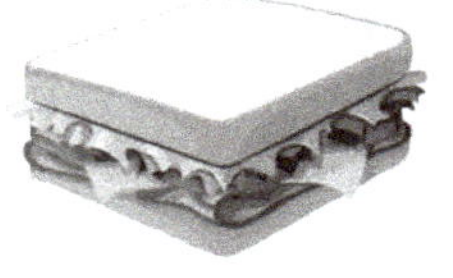
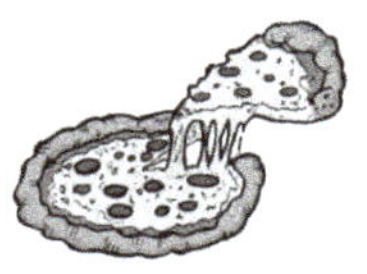

Bread	Burger	Sandwich	Pizza

8. **Desserts:** Sweet items of food eaten after the end of a meal.
   (a) **Cake** – Soft, sweet food made from flour, sugar and eggs
   (b) **Sundae** – Ice cream with fruits, chocolate sauce or dry fruits
   (c) **Kheer** – Indian sweet food made with rice and milk
   (d) **Pudding** – A cooked sweet and hot dish

Sundae	Pudding	Cake	Kheer

9. **Cutlery items:** Used for serving and eating food.
   (a) **Knife** – Used to cut food into smaller pieces
   (b) **Fork** – Used to pick up small portions of food and take it to the mouth
   (c) **Spoon** – Used to pick up small portions of food and take it to the mouth
   (d) **Plate** – Used to serve food, such as rice, vegetables curry, etc.
   (e) **Cup** – Used to serve tea or coffee
   (f) **Bowl** – Used to serve liquid food such as soup

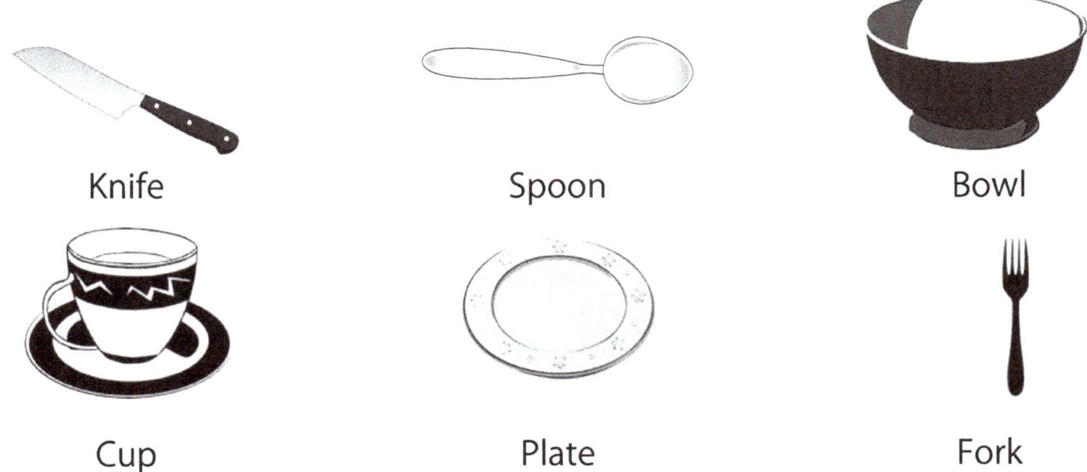

Name : _______________________________

Section : _______________

Assessment Technique:

Picture Based

Class Work

Marks : 10   Time : 20 Minutes

Directions: This is Karim's Burger corner. He makes different types of burgers. Create a menu card for him in alphabetical order.

(10 marks)

Cheese light

Simple Veg.

Veg. King size

Deluxe Non-Veg

MENU CARD

____

____

____

____

The ingredients he uses are shown below. Write the names of the missing ingredients in the space provided.

___________   ___________   Veg Cutlet   ___________   Spinach leaves

___________   ___________   Non-Veg Cutlet   ___________   Mayonnaise

Now, create your own burgers :

Cheese Light	**Simply Veg.**	**Veg King-size**	**Deluxe Non-Veg.**
__________	__________	__________	__________
__________	__________	__________	__________
__________	__________	__________	__________
__________	__________	__________	__________
__________	__________	__________	__________

Places of Religion, Worship and Holy Books

In India, people of different religions can be found. Everybody lives together here peacefully.

RELIGION

Belief and worship of God or Gods is known as religion.

There are four main religions in India.

1. **Hinduism:** People who follow Hinduism are called Hindus. They worship Gods and Goddesses like Goddess Durga, Lord Shiva, Lord Ganesha, Lord Rama.

2. **Islam:** People who follow Islam are called Muslims. They worship Allah.

3. **Sikhism:** People who follow Sikhism are called Sikhs. They worship Guru Nanak Dev.

4. **Christianity:** People who follow Christianity are called Christians. They worship Jesus Christ.

PLACES OF WORSHIP

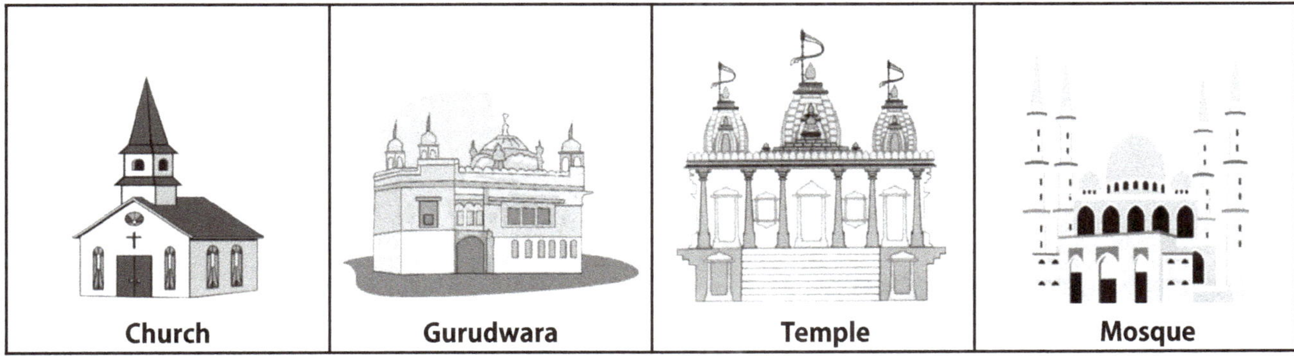

Each religion has a different place where their followers go to offer prayer and worship.

Let's learn about each one of them.

1. **Mosque:** A place where Muslims go to offer prayers is known as a Mosque.

2. **Temple:** A place where Hindus go to offer prayers is known as a Temple.

3. **Church:** A place where Christians go to offer prayers is known as a Church.

4. **Gurudwara:** A place where Sikhs go to offer prayers is known as a Gurudwara.

Guru Granth Sahib

Holy Bible

Geeta

Quran

Each religion has a special book which tells its followers how to live their life. These holy books have many good lessons to teach us.

Let's learn about them.

1. **Geeta:** The holy book of Hindus is called Geeta.
2. **Quran:** The holy book of Muslims is called Quran.
3. **Guru Granth Sahib:** The holy book of Sikhs is called Guru Granth Sahib.
4. **Bible:** The holy book of Christians is called Bible.

FESTIVALS

Holi

- Holi is a festival of colours, celebrated mostly by Hindus in North India. On this day, people play with colours and water. They throw colours at each other. It is a day when family and friends meet. They eat sweets and drink thandai (a drink made from milk and dry fruits).

Diwali

- Diwali is known as the festival of lights.
- It is celebrated because Lord Rama returned home to Ayodhya after spending 14 years in exile.
- Diwali is celebrated mostly by Hindus.
- On this day, people decorate their homes with candles and lights and worship Lord Ganesha and Goddess Lakshmi. They exchange gifts and sweets among family and friends. People also burst crackers. But one should remember that bursting crackers is not good for our surroundings.

Dussehra

- Dussehra is a festival celebrated by Hindus.

- This day marks the victory of Lord Ram over Ravana.

- People burn statues of Ravana on this day.

- This day is a symbol of victory of good over bad.

Eid-ul-Fitr

- Eid-ul-fitr or Eid is celebrated by Muslims all over the world. They fast from sunrise to sunset for one month before Eid. On the day of Eid, they offer prayers to God. It is celebrated among family and friends by eating good food, exchanging gifts known as eidis. One gets to eat delicious dishes such as Biryanis, Kebabs and Sewaiyan.

Guru Nanak Jayanti

- Guru Nanak Jayanti is a festival celebrated by Sikhs.

- It celebrates the birthday of Guru Nanak, the first Sikh Guru. People visit the Gurudwara at night and offer prayers. The Gurudwara is decorated with lights and candles.

Christmas

- Christmas is celebrated on 25th December all over the world. It is mostly celebrated by Christians. Christmas is celebrated because it is the birthday of Jesus Christ. On this day, people decorate their houses. They put up Christmas trees and decorate them. All the family members come together and exchange gifts.

Name : ______________________________

Assessment Technique:

Match Attach

Section : ______________

Class Work

Marks : 10

Time : 20 Minutes

I. Directions: Match the following. (1 × 5 = 5 marks)

Column-A		Column- B
1.	Sikhs go to the	(i)	the Muslims kneel on the floor to pray
2.	Christians have mass in	(ii)	you will find a cross
3.	In a Mosque	(iii)	a Church
4.	On top of the most of Churches	(iv)	gurudwara to worship
5.	The Hindus pray	(v)	in temples

II. Directions: Unscramble the words to reveal world religions and holy books.

(½ × 10 = 5 marks)

1. UMBDDISH   = ____

2. ISMUDNIH   = ____

3. CAYTRHINITIS = ____

4. MAILS   = ____

5. NISIMAJ   = ____

6. RANUQ   = ____

7. EEATG   = ____

8. IBLEB   = ____

9. URUGRANGTH HISAB = ____

10. JAMIDUS   = ____

CHAPTER 7

One and Many

In order to change singular (one) nouns to plural (many) nouns we add the letter 's' or 'es' at the end of the noun word.

Most singular nouns form the plural by adding **–s.**

A singular noun ending in **s, x, z, ch, sh, o** makes the plural by adding **-es.**

For example:

(a)   He is reading a **book**. (One)

He is reading three **books**. (Many)

(b)   He bought a **box** (one)

He bought six **boxes**. (Many)

Nouns which add the letter 's' at the end.

One (Singular)	Many (Plural)	One (Singular)	Many (Plural)
Car	Cars	Boy	Boys
Girl	Girls	Toy	Toys
Apple	Apples	Snake	Snakes

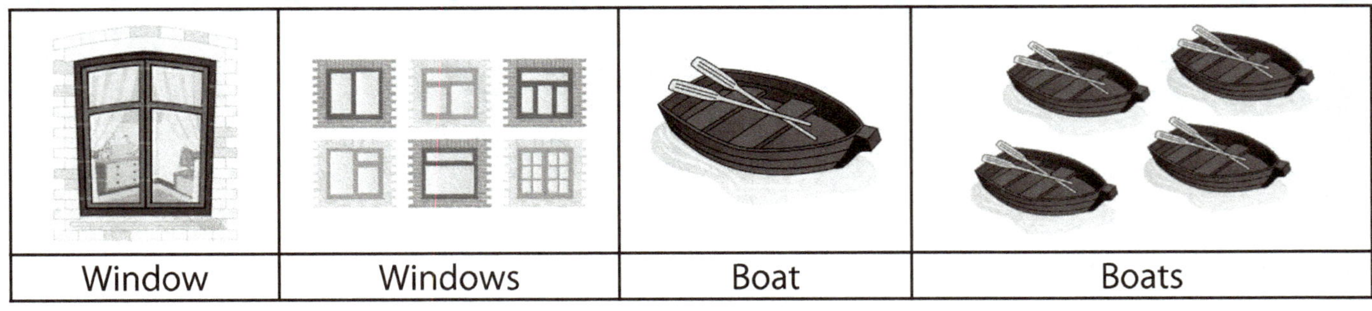

One	Many	One	Many
Window	Windows	Boat	Boats

Nouns ending in s, x, z, ch, sh, o makes the plural by adding –es.

One (Singular)	Many (Plural)	One (Singular)	Many (Plural)
Bus	Buses	Church	Churches
Box	Boxes	Potato	Potatoes
Zero	Zeroes	Axe	Axes
Brush	Brushes	Branch	Branches

Name : ________________________	Assessment Technique:
Section : ____________	**Transform Sentences**

Home Work

Marks : 10   Time : 1 Day

I. Directions: Convert the sentences using the plural of the underlined words. The sentence must be grammatically correct. (Use separate sheet.)   **(1 × 5 = 5 marks)**

1. The brown <u>box</u> has oranges in it.

    Sample Ans: The brown boxes have oranges in them.

2. The <u>girl</u> is dancing on the stage.

3. The <u>tiger</u> was chasing the <u>deer</u>.

4. The <u>child</u> loves to eat <u>ice cream</u>.

5. There is a beautiful <u>rose</u> in my garden.

II. Directions: Read the sentences given below and choose the plural form of underlined nouns from the options given below.   **(1 × 5 = 5 marks)**

1. The <u>thief</u> entered our house from the back door.

    (a) thiefs   (b) thieves   (c) theives   (d) theef

2. The <u>wolf</u> fooled the lion.

    (a) wolves   (b) wolfs   (c) wolfes   (d) wolve

3. They cut the fruits with <u>knife</u>.

    (a) knifes   (b) knives   (c) kneves   (d) knifs

4. I saw <u>monkey</u> snatching away food from people.

    (a) monkies   (b) monkeys   (c) monkys   (d) monkyies

5. The <u>baby</u> wanted to go out.

    (a) babies   (b) babys   (c) babyes   (d) babyies

CHAPTER 8

Masculine and Feminine

What is gender?

Gender can be classified into : Masculine Gender and Feminine Gender.

MASCULINE NOUNS

Masculine nouns are words used for men, boys and male animals.

FEMININE NOUNS

Feminine nouns are words which are used for women, girls, and female animals.

List of Masculine and Feminine Nouns:

Masculine	Feminine	Masculine	Feminine	Masculine	Feminine
Boy	Girl	Hero	Heroine	Man	Woman
Waiter	Waitress	Bride	Bridegroom	Brother	Sister
Father	Mother	King	Queen	Prince	Princess
Actor	Actress	God	Goddess	Grandfather	Grandmother
Husband	Wife	Sir	Madam	Son	Daughter
Uncle	Aunt	Nephew	Niece	Policeman	Policewoman

Some nouns are used for both males and females. These nouns are known as common gender nouns.

1. Child
2. Friend
3. Guest
4. Owner
5. Singer
6. Cat
7. Parent
8. Student
9. Baby
10. Bird

GENDER FOR ANIMALS

Animal	Masculine	Feminine	Animal	Masculine	Feminine
Ass	Jack	Jenny	Chicken	Cock	Hen
Deer	Buck	Doe	Dog	Dog	Bitch
Duck	Drake	Duck	Goose	Gander	Goose
Lion	Lion	Lioness	Tiger	Tiger	Tigress
Horse	Stallion	Mare	Cattle	Bull	Cow
Bear	Bear	She-bear	Peacock	Peacock	Peahen
Pig	Boar	Sow			

Name : _________________________

Section : _____________

Assessment Technique:

Gender Conversion

I.   Directions: Write the opposite gender of the following.   (½ × 10 = 5 marks)

1. Son: _________________   6.   Bride: _________________

2. Madam: _________________   7.   King: _________________

3. Peacock: _________________   8.   Horse: _________________

4. Priest: _________________   9.   Headmaster: _________________

5. Washerman: _________________   10. Poet: _________________

II. Directions: Rewrite the following sentences after changing the genders. (Use separate sheet.)   (½ × 10 = 5 marks)

1.   My brother is good at studies.

2.   Vishnu's grandfather tells him stories at bed time.

3.   The waiter was very polite.

4.   His nephew is a famous artist.

5.   Reshma's father is a manager in a bank.

6.   My aunt bought me a beautiful leather jacket.

7.   The tiger attacked the animals.

8.   The actor is also a good singer.

9.   The prince went hunting in the jungle.

10.   The hero was riding on a motorcycle.

One Word Substitution

What do we mean by the word 'substitution'?
Substitution means replacing one thing with another.
For example:
I do not like **peas.**
Let's substitute the word 'peas' with 'tomatoes'.
I do not like **tomatoes.**
Now let us learn about one word substitutions.
When we replace many words with just one word without changing the meaning of those words, it is known as one word substitution.
For example:
(a) I go to the place **where flowers and grass grow** every evening.
Now, let us replace the words in bold with something more fitting.
Flowers and grass grow in a garden, so now the sentence will be:
I go to the **garden** every evening.
(b) I have to visit the **doctor who takes care of teeth.**
Now let us replace the words in bold with one word.
A doctor who takes care of teeth is known as a dentist, so now the sentence will be:
I have to visit the **dentist**.

VOCABULARY

Let us learn a few new words.

King: A ruler of a place or an area is called a king.	**Queen:** The king's wife is called a queen.
Prince: The king's son is called a prince.	**Princess:** The king's daughter is called a princess.

Kingdom: The area which is ruled by the king is called kingdom.	**Palace:** The king's home is called a palace.
Crown: The ornament worn by a king on the head is called a crown.	**Throne:** The chair on which the king sits is called a throne.
Sword: The weapon with which a king fights is called a sword.	**Fairy:** An imaginary person who can do magic.
Wand: The magic stick with which a fairy does magic.	**Wings:** Used to fly

Fairy tale: A make believe story which does not happen in real world. It will often tell us about imaginary creatures like fairies and dragons that do not exist in the real world.

Name : _______________________

Assessment Technique:

Crossword

Section : ____________

Home Work

Marks : 10

Time : 1 Day

I. Directions: Identify the people who do things for us and complete the crossword.

(½ × 10 = 5 marks)

Across	**Down**

Across

3. A person who mends shoes.

5. A person who sells meat.

7. A person who sells fruits and vegetables

8. A person who travels in space.

9. A person who draws and plans a building.

10. A person who sells medicine.

Down

1. A person who looks after sheep.

2. A person who sells flowers.

4. A person who makes things of iron.

6. A person who drives a motor car.

II. Directions: Match the following.   (½ × 10 = 5 marks)

Column A	Column B
1. A place were aeroplanes are kept.	(i) Witch
2. A bunch of flowers.	(ii) Library
3. A group of fish.	(iii) Wardrobe
4. A book containing words and their meanings.	(iv) Troupe
5. Feminine of wizard.	(v) Orchestra
6. A room where you will find lots of books.	(vi) Swarm
7. A place to keep clothes.	(vii) Dictionary
8. A group of dancers.	(viii) Hanger
9. A group of musicians.	(ix) Bouquet
10. A group of bees.	(x) School

CHAPTER 10

Pronouns

A pronoun is a word that takes the place of a noun. Noun is the name of a person, place, thing or animal.

It is a short word which can be used instead of the name of the noun. Pronouns are very helpful because if you use them, you do not need to write the name of the noun again and again.

For example:

Ram has a dog. **He** likes the dog very much. **It** has puppies. **They** are very small.

Ram is a noun. We can use **'he'** in the place of Ram.

Dog is a noun. We can use **'it'** in the place of dog.

Puppies are plural. So we can use **'they'** in the place of puppies.

Some common pronouns are:

1.	He	**2.**	She	**3.**	It	**4.**	I
5.	We	**6.**	They	**7.**	Us	**8.**	You

TYPES OF PRONOUNS

1.	Personal pronoun	**2.**	Possessive pronoun

1. Personal pronoun

A personal pronoun describes:

- The person who is speaking (I, We, Us).

For example:

(a) **I** am going to eat. *Only 'I' or one person is going to eat.*

(b) **We** are going to eat. *More than one person are going to eat.*

For example:

(a) Are **you** coming? *Someone is asking the other person if he or she will come.*

(b) Will **you** go? *Someone is asking the other person if her or she will go.*

- The person or thing or group spoken about (he, she, it, they).

For example:

(a) Maya is a good girl. She dances well. *The pronoun **"she"** is a personal pronoun, describing a particular person (Maya) who dances well.*

(b) My neighbour has a dog. It barks a lot. *The pronoun 'it' is a personal pronoun, describing a particular thing (dog) who barks a lot.*

2. Possessive Pronoun

Possessive Pronouns in English

It shows the relationship of a thing or person to another thing or person.

For example: yours, mine, his, hers, theirs

- **Yours** is used to show something that belongs to the person spoken to.
  For example:
  (a) This book belongs to you.
  This book is **yours**. (Possessive pronoun)

- **Mine** is used to show something that belongs to me.
  For example:
  (a) This book belongs to me.
  This book is **mine**. (Possessive pronoun)

- His, hers, and theirs are used to show something that belongs to a man/boy, woman/girl or a group of people.
  For example:
  (a) This book belongs to **him**. (Man/Boy)
  This book is **his**. (Possessive Pronoun)

Name : ________________________

Section : ____________

Assessment Technique:

Application Based Worksheet

Home Work

Marks : 20   Time : 1 Day

I.   Directions : Given below are some sentences without pronouns. You need to fill in the blanks with correct pronouns.   **(1 × 10 = 10 marks)**

1.   Vijay is reading books and _____________ friends are playing.

2.   _____________ are going to watch a movie.

3.   Rita looks much prettier than _____________ sister.

4.   Rahul and _____________ brother are going to meet _____________ grandparents.

5.   Rohan is a mail carrier. _____________ carries a blue bag.

6.   _____________ went to the store with Anshika. After shopping, _____________ both had lunch.

7.   When the Sun comes up, _____________ all leave for work.

8.   Sunny is a good cook. _____________ made dinner for the whole family.

9.   Mr. Sharma went to the movie with _____________ wife in _____________ new car.

10. Have _____________ seen the sandcastle _____________ built?

II. Directions: Read the following stories carefully and fill in the blanks with suitable pronouns.   **(1 × 10 = 10 marks)**

STORY

(i)______ was summer vacation. Suresh was feeling very bored. (ii)______ decided to play in the garden. Even as (iii)______ was throwing his ball towards the wall, (iv)________________ heard a loud thud. The thud was followed by a shout. (v)______ looked upwards. A lady was looking out of a broken window.

(vi)______ was looking very angry. The old windowpanes were broken. (vii)______ was a sorry sight. Suresh was so frightened that (viii)______ ran away. The angry lady was waving (ix)______ hands. The broken part of the window fell on (x)______ head. (xi)______ fell back in fright.

Name : ______________________________

Section : ________________

Assessment Technique:

Fillers

Class Work

Marks : 20   Time : 25 Minutes

I. Directions : Choose the correct pronouns from the brackets and fill in the blanks.

(1 × 10 = 10 marks)

1. Manu said that ______________ likes to eat an ice cream (he/they)

2. Anu is Maya's best friend. ______________ play together (They/She)

3. Manya bought a dog. ______________ is very naughty. (She/It)

4. I don't like cold drinks. Give ______________ lemonade. (it/me)

5. Why don't ______________ accompany us? (he/you)

6. Shruti loves her grandma. ______________ goes to the park with her. (Her/She)

7. Sanya is my neighbour. She lost ______________ bag. (her/she)

8. This is a tree. ______________ was planted by my grandfather. (He/It)

9. ______________ am going to Chari's house. (We/ I)

10. The teacher is giving ______________ a ball. (we/us)

II. Directions : Rewrite the following sentences by changing the underlined nouns into pronouns.

(1 × 10 = 10 marks)

1. The traveller rode the <u>traveller's</u> horse as fast as the <u>horse</u> could go.

2. Ritu said that <u>Ritu</u> wanted to read <u>Ritu's</u> favourite poem to Sunny and Stuti.

3. Sunny and Stuti enjoyed the poem that Ritu read to <u>Sunny and Stuti.</u>

4. Sunny is Ritu's best friend, so <u>Sunny</u> went to the store with <u>Ritu.</u>

5. Varun and Vicky are brothers. <u>Varun and Vicky</u> will go together to watch movie.

6. Pooja and Mohan are in the park. <u>Pooja and Mohan</u> are playing.

7. Rakshita and I are going to the market. <u>Rakshita and I</u> will buy few dresses.

Action Words

Verbs are known as "action words". They describe actions. Action verbs tell us what people or things are doing.

Here are Some Common Action Verbs

Drink   Look   Jump   Swim   Fall   Eat   Shout   Walk

Throw   Climb   Laugh   Run   Sit   Catch   Dance

Examples of verbs used in sentences

(a)   Ripu **climbs** a mountain. (*The word 'climbs' is a verb. It tells us what Ripu is doing.*)

(b)   Shanu likes to **swim.** (*The word 'swim' is a verb. It tells us what Shanu likes to do.*)

(c)   Rita is **eating** lunch. (*The word 'eating' is a verb. It tells us what Rita is doing.*)

(d)   Mr. Sharma **drives** a car. (*The word 'drives' is a verb. It tells us what Mr. Sharma does.*)

(e)   We will **walk** in the evening. (*The word 'walk' is a verb. It tells us what 'we' will do in the evening.*)

Name : _______________________

Section : _____________

Assessment Technique:

MCQ Based Worksheet

Home Work

Marks : 20

Time : 1 Day

I.   Directions : Choose the best answer.   **(1 × 12 = 12 marks)**

1. The Sun _______________ in the morning.

    (a)   rise   (b)   rises   (c)   risen

2. Randhir _______________ to play chess.

    (a)   love   (b)   loves   (c)   loving

3. The cat _______________ after the rat.

    (a)   ran   (b)   run   (c)   running

4. Sujata likes to _______________ story books.

    (a)   read   (b)   reads   (c)   reading

5. Ramu and Rani are always _______________with each other.

    (a)   fight   (b)   fights   (c)   fighting.

6. The crowd _______________ mad with joy when our team won the match.

    (a)   go   (b)   went   (c)   gone

7. The monkey _______________ from branch to branch.

    (a)   leap   (b)   leapt   (c)   leaping

8. The magic pencil _______________ a colourful scooter.

    (a)   draw   (b)   drew   (c)   drawn

9. He _______________ a balloon with his bubble gum.

    (a)   blow   (b)   blew   (c)   blown

10. ______________________ you do your homework by yourself ?

   (a)   Is   (b)   Did   (c)   Does

11. The little bird had ______________________ off from the nest.

   (a)   fell   (b)   fall   (c)   fallen

12. Ritik has ______________________ to bring his maths homework.

   (a)   forget   (b)   forgot   (c)   forgotten

II. **Directions: Complete the sentences given below by choosing the correct verb from the given options. Look at the pictures carefully before selecting the verbs. (1 × 8 = 8 marks)**

1. The pretty girl was ______________ on the stage.
   (a) dancing   (b) laughing   (c) kicking

2. The cricket ball ______________ the window pane.
   (a) closed   (b) split   (c) shattered

3. The little girl was ______________ in the garden.
   (a) walking   (b) hopping   (c) jogging

4. The bird ______________ its wings and soared high up in the sky.
   (a) swooped   (b) spread   (c) glided

5. The tree was ______________ in the wind.
   (a) growing   (b) swaying   (c) spreading

6. The Holi festival is _________________ every year at his place.

   (a) held   (b) performed   (c) celebrated

7. The boy was _____________ on his bike.

   (a) galloping   (b) driving   (c) riding

8. The lady was ______________ yoga early in the morning.

   (a) doing   (b) playing   (c) working

CHAPTER 12

Helping Verbs

IS, AM, ARE, WAS, AND WERE

Helping verbs are words that help the main verb in a sentence. With their help, the meaning of the sentence becomes clearer.

Some common helping verbs are: **Is, am, are, was, were.**

Let's learn how to use these helping verbs:

I, am, are,was, were are helping verbs which tell us about the state of the main verb, that is if the main action word is singular or plural, in present tense or past tense.

1. **Am** – Am is always used with the pronoun 'I' .
   For example:
   (a) I *am* **running**.
   (b) I *am* **eating**.
   (c) I *am* not **well**.
   (d) I *am* **sad**.

2. **Is and Are** – **Is** and **are** are used to show that the action being done is in the present tense.
   Is – used for singular nouns and pronouns. (One)
   Are – used for plural nouns and pronouns. (Many)
   For example:
   (a) We *are* going to the market. (Many)
   (b) He *is* going to the market. (One)
   (c) Radha *is* dancing. (One)
   (d) They *are* shouting. (Many)
   (e) The boys *are* eating. (Many)
   (f) Joy *is* swimming. (One)
   (g) Pink and Cheeku *are* going to school. (Many)

HAS, HAD, HAVE

The helping verbs has, had and have are used to show ownership.

Now let's learn how to use them.

1. **Has** – Has is used to show ownership of something in the present tense. It is used with pronouns – he, she, it and with singular nouns.
   For example:
   (a) He **has** a cold.
   (b) She **has** a new haircut.
   (c) It **has** a hole.
   (d) It **has** not moved.
   (e) She **has** a pretty smile.

2. **Have** - Have is also used to show ownership of something in the present tense. It is used with pronouns – I, you, we, they – and with plural nouns.
    For example:
    (a) I **have** lots of books.
    (b) They **have** no food.
    (c) We **have** to leave now.
    (d) You **have** something on your face.
    (e) Soldiers **have** a tough job.
3. **Had** – Had is used to show ownership of something in the past tense.
    It is used for both singular and plural nouns and all pronouns – I, we, you, they, he, she, it.
    For example:
    (a) I **had** a dog.
    (b) We **had** lots of books.
    (c) Radha **had** good hair.
    (d) It **had** less fur.
    (e) You **had** a lot of homework.

CAN, MAY, WILL

Can, may and will are helping verbs which help in changing the meaning of the main action word/verb.
Let's learn how to use can, may, will.
1. **Can** – The helping verb 'can' is used to express ability of a person or thing to do something.
    For example:
    (a) He **can** dance.
    (b) She **can** sing.
    (c) It **can** bark loudly.
    (d) We **can** run.
    (e) You **can** go.
2. **May** – The helping verb 'may' is used to take permission
    For example:
    (a) **May** I go to the washroom?
    (b) **May** I borrow your pen?
    (c) **May** we go out?
    (d) **May** we have dinner early?
3. **Will** – The helping verb 'will' is used to express willingness or wish to do something.
    For example:
    (a) I **will** visit my grandmother.
    (b) She **will** do her homework.
    (c) He **will** not eat lunch today.
    (d) You **will** be late.
    (e) They **will** go for a trip.

Name : _______________________	Assessment Technique:
Section : _______________	**MCQ Based Worksheet**

Home Work

Marks : 10 | Time : 1 Day

Directions: Choose the best answer to fill in the blanks. (1 × 10 = 10 marks)

1. The boy _____________________ roaming in the garden.
   (a) an   (b) was
   (c) are   (d) were

2. Rakesh _____________________ playing with his friends.
   (a) is   (b) were
   (c) was   (d) (a) & (c)

3. The girls _____________________ going for a movie.
   (a) is   (b) were
   (c) was   (d) am

4. I _____________________ preparing for tomorrow's picnic.
   (a) is   (b) am
   (c) was   (d) (b) & (c)

5. Anamika _____________________ working hard for her dance show.
   (a) are   (b) was
   (c) were   (d) none of these

6. Rita _____________________ been learning music since the age of six.
   (a) has   (b) had
   (c) have   (d) (a) & (b)

7. Rajesh _____________________ been a computer freak even as a young boy.
   (a) has   (b) have
   (c) had   (d) (a) & (c)

8. We _____________________ been a part of the school choir for several years.
   (a) has   (b) was
   (c) have   (d) were

9. You _____________________ been working too hard.
   (a) has   (b) have
   (c) were   (d) was

10. They _____________________ gone on a long vacation to the Andamans.
   (a) has   (b) are
   (c) had   (d) were

Name : _______________________

Section : _____________

Assessment Technique:

Fillers

Class Work

Marks : 10   **Time : 30 Minutes**

Directions: Fill in the blanks with "has" and "have".   (1 × 10 = 10 marks)

1.   A butterfly _____________________________ beautiful wings.

2.   The girls _____________________________ new dolls.

3.   She _____________________________ curly hair.

4.   The old lady _____________________________ a big umbrella.

5.   An elephant _____________________________ big ears.

6.   You _____________________________ a beautiful smile.

7.   He_____________________________ to go out.

8.   I _____________________________ a bad cold.

9.   I _____________________________ a test today.

10. A parrot _____________________________ a red beak.

CHAPTER 13

Rhyming Words

Fin

Bin

Pin

Win

What is common in the words given above?
They all end with the same sound **'in'**.

RHYMING WORDS

Rhyming words are words that end with the same sound.
For example: Hot, Pot, Lot – sound of **'ot'** is the same in all three words.

Please note: In rhyming words, only the sound at the end of the word should match, not the spelling.

Cat	Hat

List of Common Rhyming Words

- **Words ending with 'ad'**

  Mad   Sad   Bad   Lad   Glad   Had   Pad   Dad

- **Words ending with 'ag'**

  Bag   Drag   Rag

- **Words ending with 'am'**

  Am   Jam   Sam   Pam   Slam

- **Words ending with 'at'**

  Cat   Mat   Hat   Rat   Pat   That   Sat

- **Words ending with 'an'**

Pan   Can   Van   Man   Fan   Than

- **Words ending with 'ap'**

Gap   Lap   Nap   Map   Trap   Cap   Tap

- **Words ending with 'ed'**

Bed   Shed   Led   Red   Wed

- **Words ending with 'en'**

Pen   Hen   Men   Den   Then   When   Ten

- **Words ending with 'et'**

Get   Pet   Met   Jet   Yet   Let

- **Words ending with 'un'**

Fun   Bun   Run   Gun   Sun

- **Words ending with 'ut'**

But   Nut   Cut   Hut

Name : ________________________

Section : ____________

Assessment Technique:

Choose and Colour

Class Work

Marks : 10 | Time : 20 Minutes

I. **Directions: Colour the word that rhymes with the given word.** **(½ × 10 = 5 marks)**

1.	Light	:	sight	bright	feat
2.	glass	:	glove	class	grass
3.	goat	:	coat	broke	boat
4.	bubble	:	puddle	double	tack
5.	home	:	dome	foam	grown
6.	spoon	:	spool	toon	moon
7.	house	:	mouse	louse	grows
8.	head	:	bed	bread	bead
9.	shop	:	hop	cup	crop
10.	best	:	rest	beast	nest

II. **Directions: Match the words with the words that rhyme with them. (½ × 10 = 5 marks)**

	Column A		Column B
1.	owl	(i)	shook
2.	cow	(ii)	fist
3.	bull	(iii)	hip
4.	yellow	(iv)	put
5.	book	(v)	sand
6.	mist	(vi)	late
7.	ship	(vii)	growl
8.	foot	(viii)	now
9.	band	(ix)	pull
10.	gate	(x)	fellow

Describing Words & Comparison of Adjectives

ADJECTIVES OR DESCRIBING WORDS

Adjectives describe the quality of nouns and pronouns. They tell us more about size, shape, colour or number of people, places, things or animals.

Describing words are of different types.

Some adjectives tell about the size of people or things.

(a)   A **big** house

(b)   **Tiny** feet

(c)   A **high** mountain

(d)   A **large** army

(e)   **Big** hands

Some adjectives tell about the colour of things.

(a)   A **red** car

(b)   A **black** suit

(c)   A **brown** bear

Some adjectives tell what people or things are like by telling us their quality.

(a)   A **beautiful** scene

(b)   A **young** man

(c)   An **old** aunt

(d)   A **hot** drink

(e)   A **cold** day

Adjectives can be written in three different forms to compare an object/person with the other – **positive, comparative and superlative.**
Now let's learn about each form.

- **The Positive**

  When we speak about one person, thing, animal or place, we use the positive form.

  For example:

  (a) This car is **small**.

  In this sentence only one noun (This car) is being talked about. So, we use the positive form of adjective 'small'.

  (b) He is a **tall** student.

  In this sentence only one person (He) is being talked about. So, we use the positive form of adjective 'tall'.

- **The Comparative**

  To compare two people, things, places or animals, we use the comparative form of the adjective. The comparative form is usually made by adding 'er' to the end of the adjective.

  > **Please note:** We use the word 'than' in comparative sentences.

  For example:

  (a) This car is bigger than my father's car.

  In this sentence two nouns are being talked about (This car and father's car). So, we use the comparative form of adjective 'bigger'.

  (b) He is taller than Ajay.

  In this sentence two persons are being talked about (He and Ajay). So, we use the comparative form of adjective 'taller'.

- **The Superlative**

  When we compare three or more people or things, we use the superlative form of the adjective. The superlative form is usually made by adding 'est' to the adjective.

  > **Please note:** We often add 'the' before the superlative form of the adjective.

  For example:

  (a) Shyam is **tall**. (Positive)

  Rohan is **taller** than Shyam. (Comparative)

  Raj is the **tallest** in the class. (Superlative)

(b) This car is **big**. (positive)

This car is **bigger** than my father's. (comparative)

This car is the **biggest** in our city. (superlative)

List of adjectives in positive, comparative and superlative form.

Positive	Comparative (add "er")	Superlative (add "est")
Dark	Darker	Darkest
Hard	Harder	Hardest
Light	Lighter	Lightest
Warm	Warmer	Warmest
High	Higher	Highest
Cold	Colder	Coldest
Low	Lower	Lowest
Fast	Faster	Fastest
Old	Older	Oldest
Slow	Slower	Slowest
Young	Younger	Youngest
Rich	Richer	Richest
Poor	Poorer	Poorest
Tall	Taller	Tallest
Small	Smaller	Smallest
Soft	Softer	Softest
Nice	Nicer	Nicest
Close	Closer	Closest
Long	Longer	Longest
Sad	Sadder	Saddest
Cheerful	More Cheerful	Most Cheerful
Foolish	More foolish	Most foolish
Little	Less	Least
Good	Better	Best
Up	Upper	Uppermost

Name : _______________________

Section : _____________

Assessment Technique:

Identification Based

Marks : 20

Time : 1 Day

I.   Directions: Underline the nouns and circle adjectives in the given sentences.

(1 × 10 = 10 marks)

1. We are going on an exciting trip to Disneyland.
2. Children like to watch the interesting cartoons.
3. The famous magician brought out colourful hankies from his hat.
4. Ravish dreamt that he defeated the powerful wrestlers in the WWF.
5. The expensive vase with colourful flowers looked beautiful.
6. Radhika's little cupboard is full of electronic toys.
7. The careless boy poured hot milk over himself.
8. My grandmother lives in a big house with a beautiful garden.
9. The huge giant hugged the little boy.
10. The giant spaceship landed in a lonely park.

II.   Directions: Give two adjectives for each of the following Nouns. (1 × 10 = 10 marks)

1.	Mahatma Gandhi	__________	__________
2.	River Ganges	__________	__________
3.	McDonald's	__________	__________
4.	Ben 10	__________	__________
5.	Abdul Kalam	__________	__________

6.	Barbie		
7.	Taj Mahal		
8.	Himalayas		
9.	Movie 'Singham'		
10.	Mother Teresa		

Name : _______________________

Section : _____________

Assessment Technique:

Degree Comparisons Based

Class Work

Marks : 10

Time : 15 Minutes

Directions: Write the different degrees of adjectives in the table given below.

$(1 \times 10 = 10$ marks$)$

		Comparative	Superlative
1.	Clean		
2.	Tall		
3.	Slow		
4.	Heavy		
5.	Cheerful		
6.	Little		
7.	Old		
8.	Beautiful		
9.	Difficult		
10.	White		

Opposites

A word that is completely different in meaning to another word is called its opposite.

For example:

Hot – Cold   Thin - Fat

List of Common Opposite Words

Good – bad	Always – never
Alive – dead	Awake – asleep
White – black	Before – after
Boy – girl	In – out
Day – night	Sit – stand
Up - down	East –west
Early – late	Easy – hard
Empty – full	First – last
True – false	Love – hate
Friend – enemy	Go – stop

Name : ___________________________

Assessment Technique:

Section : _____________

Reverse Converse

Home Work

Marks : 20

Time : 1 Day

I. **Directions: Give the opposites of the following words.** (1 × 10 = 10 marks)

1. Left : ___________________
2. Few : ___________________
3. Old : ___________________
4. Late : ___________________
5. Under : ___________________
6. Biggest : ___________________
7. Always : ___________________
8. Difficult : ___________________
9. Clean : ___________________
10. Pull : ___________________

II. **Directions: Complete the following sentences by using the opposites of the underlined words.** (1 × 10 = 10 marks)

1. Suraj was ___________ last week. Now he looks <u>healthy</u>.

2. I was a <u>short</u> boy in class 1. Now I have grown ___________ .

3. The first question was <u>easy</u> but the next two are _______.

4. The crow was <u>clever</u> but the dog was ___________ .

5.  Rahul is having a <u>hot</u> tea but his sister is eating _______ ice cream.

6. Mahesh is very ___________ whereas Ratan is <u>thin</u> .

7.  This glass is ___________ but the other one is <u>full</u> of water.

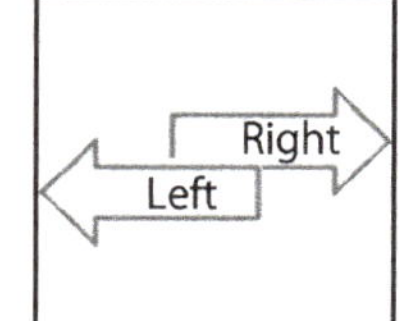

8. Sheetal is going to ___________ side but Meetal is going to <u>left</u>.

9. 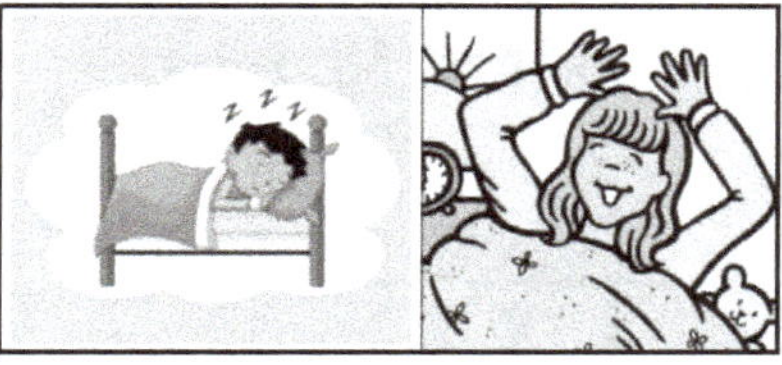 Raman is ___________ while Ritu is <u>awake</u>.

10. Neha's room is very ___________ but your's is <u>untidy</u>.

CHAPTER 16

This, That, Those, These

The words **this, that, these** and **those** are special pronouns. They are used to point out a person or thing.

Let's learn how to use this, that, these and those.

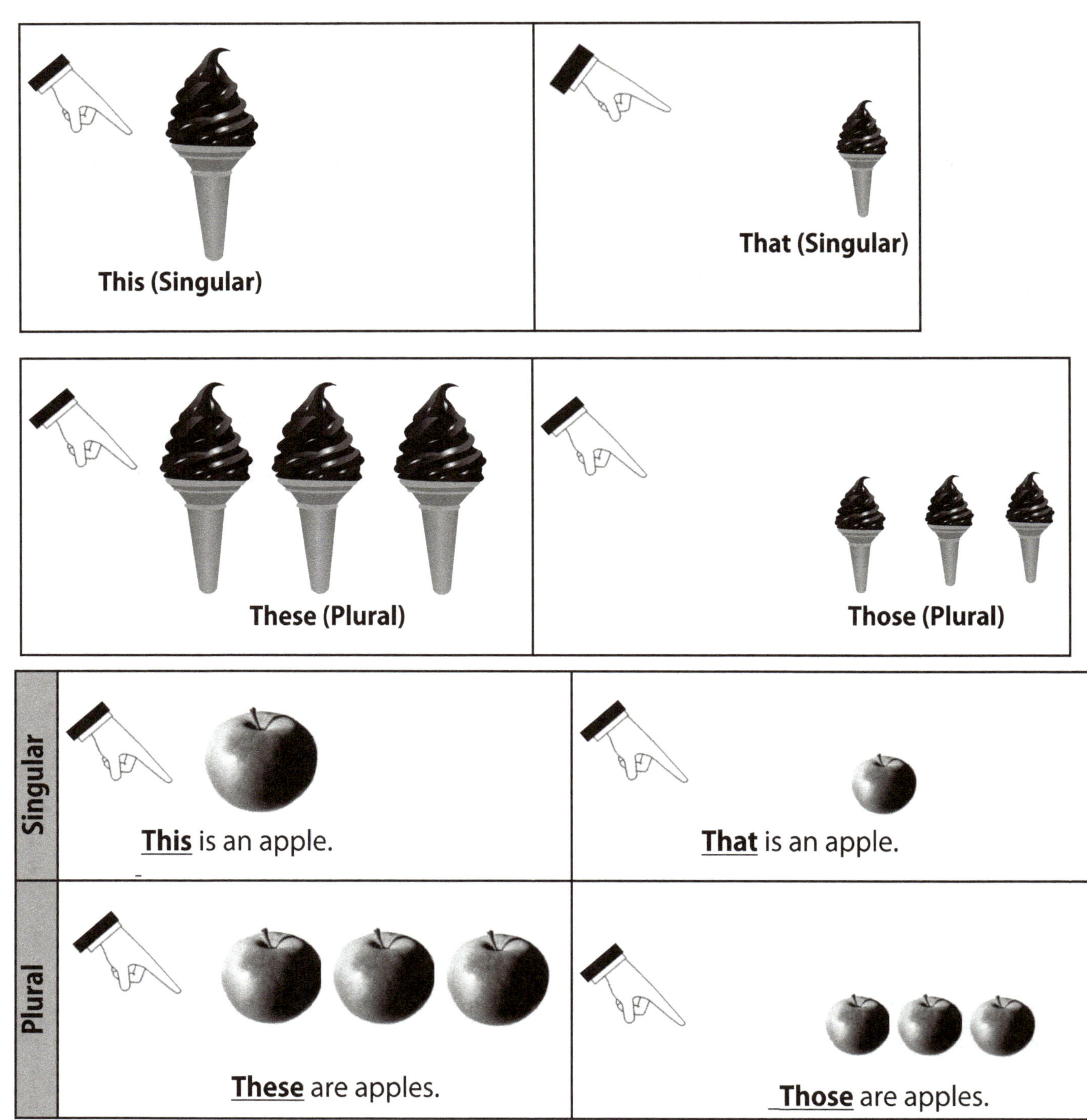

- Use **this** and **these** to talk about things and people that are near you.
- Use **this** with singular nouns.
- Use **these** with plural nouns.

For example:

(a)   I live in **this** house.

(b)   **This** car belongs to my father.

(c)   **These** keys are mine.

(d)   **These** clothes look dirty.

(e)   **This** man is my uncle.

THAT AND THOSE

- Use **that** and **those** to talk about things that are farther away from you.
- Use **that** with singular nouns
- Use **those** with plural nouns.

For example:

(a)   This book is mine and **that** book is yours.

(b)   **That** man looks funny.

(c)   Can you pass me **those** oranges?

(d)   I gave my pens to **those** boys.

(e)   These shoes are mine and **those** shoes are yours.

Name : _________________________

Assessment Technique:

Section : _____________

Fillers

Home Work

Marks : 20   Time : 1 Day

I.   **Directions: Choose the right option to fill in the blanks.**   **(1 × 10 = 10 marks)**

1. ______________ city is known as the city of joy.
   (a) This   (b)   Those   (c) These

2. ______________ mangoes are simply delicious.
   (a) That   (b)   These   (c) This

3. I would love to go to ______________ famous retreat.
   (a) those   (b)   these   (c) that

4. ______________ children are going to school.
   (a) Those   (b)   That   (c) This

5. __________________ medicines are very good for your health.
   (a) That   (b)   These   (c) This

6. __________________ are very strange creatures.
   (a) Those   (b)   This   (c) That

7. He told me to look at __________________ UFO.
   (a) these   (b)   those   (c) that

8. __________________ stadium is well maintained.
   (a) Those   (b)   This   (c) These

9. Do you see ______________ bird over there?
   (a) those   (b)   that   (c) this

10. ______________ shoes are hurting me.
   (a) That   (b)   This   (c) These

II.   **Directions: Choose the correct form for each sentence.**   **(1 × 10 = 10 marks)**

1. Can you move ______________ books into the other room? (those/them)
2. Please pass me ______________ cards. (that/those)
3. I have to take ______________ DVDs back to the store. (these/that)
4. ______________ airport is 50 miles away from here. (This/That)
5. May I borrow some of ______________ boxes? (these/that)
6. Look at ______________ plane flying high above us. (this/that)
7. ______________ is my favourite type of ice cream. (These/This)
8. I don't know any of ______________ people. (those/them)
9. ______________ mice are so cute! (These/That)
10. I don't know where the files are. I haven't seen ______________. (those/them)

Compound Words

Compound words *are formed when two or more words are joined together to form a new word with new meaning.*

For example :

Base + Ball = **Baseball**
Grand + Father = **Grandfather**
Moon + Light = **Moonlight**

Let's learn a few more compound words.

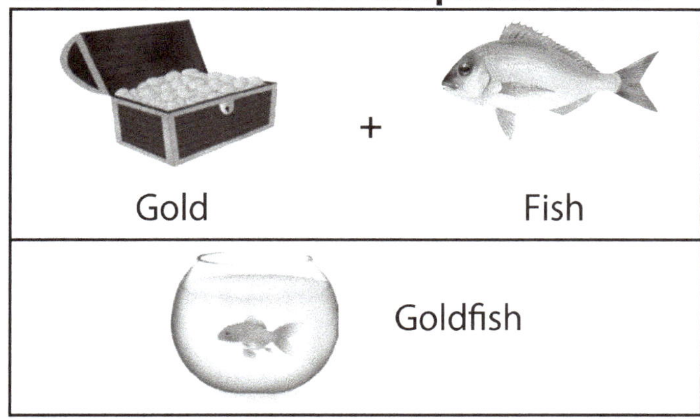

Gold + Fish

Goldfish

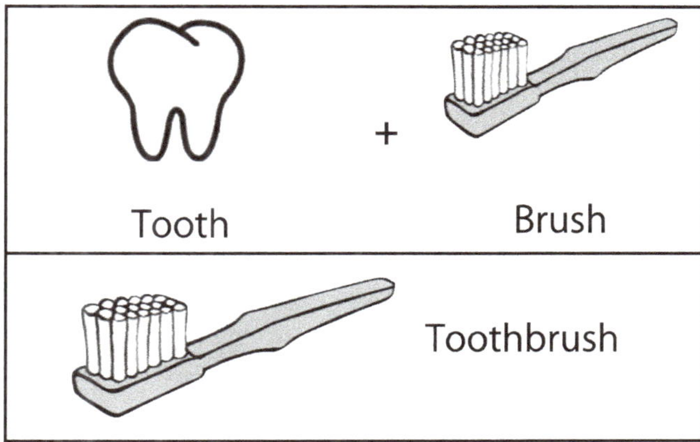

Tooth + Brush

Toothbrush

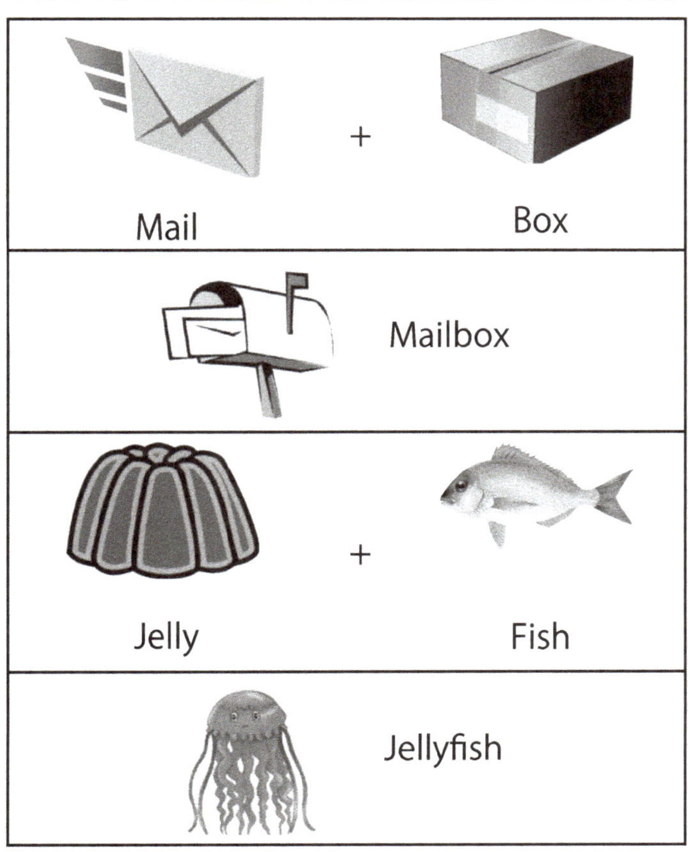

Mail + Box

Mailbox

Jelly + Fish

Jellyfish

Arm + Chair

Armchair

Dog + House

Doghouse

Pan + Cake

Pancake

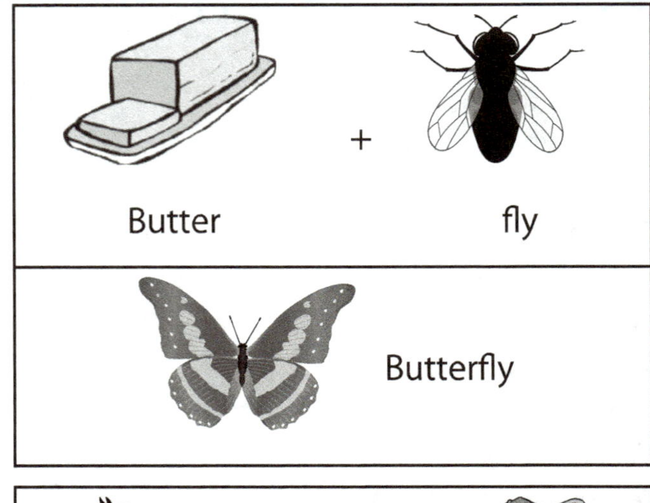

Butter + fly

Butterfly

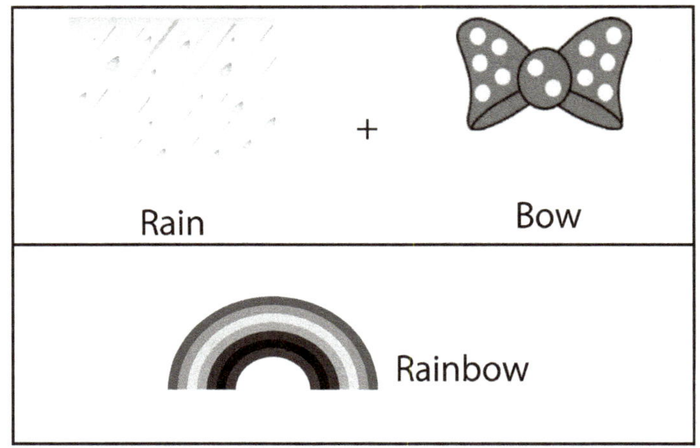

Rain + Bow

Rainbow

Horse + Shoe

Horseshoe

Tea + Pot

Teapot

Name : _______________________

Section : _____________

Assessment Technique:

Fillers

Home Work

Marks : 20   Time : 1 Day

I. **Directions: Add the two words to make compound words. Then use them in the blanks given below.** (½ × 20 = 10 marks)

1. star + fish = _____________________	6. super + natural = __________________
2. wall + paper = __________________	7. thanks + giving = ________________
3. rattle + snake = ________________	8. flash + light = ______________
4. space + ship = ________________	9. wild + life = __________________
5. scare + crow = ________________	10. mail + box = ______________

1. There was no electricity so we used a ____.

2. In USA, people thank each other on _____________________________ day.

3. A _________________________________ is shaped like a star.

4. The paint of the room is wearing off. It requires a new __________________.

5. I got scared when I saw a _________________________________ in the bushes.

6. The _______________________ landed on the moon.

7. The _____________________ is used in the fields to scare away the birds.

8. India has many _____________________ sanctuaries for animals.

9. We saw a movie based on _____________________ events.

10. On my birthday my _____________________ was flooded with mails.

II. **Directions: Make new words by pairing them from column A and B. Write the new words formed in the space provided. One has been done for you.**

(1 × 10 = 10 marks)

Column A		**Column B**	
1. butter	(i)	fly	(a) <u>butterfly</u>
2. horse	(ii)	hopper	(b) _______________
3. super	(iii)	board	(c) _______________
4. black	(iv)	cream	(d) _______________
5. ink	(v)	light	(e) _______________
6. railway	(vi)	sheet	(f) _______________
7. sun	(vii)	pot	(g) _______________
8. rain	(viii)	cart	(h) _______________
9. bed	(ix)	station	(i) _______________
10. ice	(x)	bow	(j) _______________
11. grass	(xi)	man	(k) _______________

CHAPTER 18

Punctuation Marks

Punctuation marks are signs which are added at the end or in the middle of the sentence to make the meaning clear. They are periods, commas and question marks.

PERIOD

Put a period at the end of a sentence.
For example:
(a)   It is a sunny day.
(b)   We are going out.
(c)   Shivam likes ice cream.

COMMA

A comma can be used in many ways.
Let's learn how to use a comma.
1.   Put a comma between items in a list.
     For example:
     (a) We need bread, eggs, milk and fruit.
     (b) She likes reading, swimming, playing and running.
2.   Put a comma after yes and no.
     For example:
     (a) Do you like cakes?   -   Yes, I like it very much.
     (b) Is this your pen?   -   Yes, it is.

QUESTION MARK

Use a question mark at the end of a sentence which asks a question.
For example:
(a) Can you see anything?
(b) Are we going out?

CAPITALIZATION

Use a capital letter for:
1.   The first letter of every new sentence.
2.   The first letter of names of people.
3.   The first letter of names of places, rivers, mountains.
4.   The letter "I" when it is written on its own is always capitalized.
For example:
(a)   you are mad. – incorrect
      You are mad. – correct
(b)   sheetal, cheeku and tina are my best friends – incorrect

      Sheetal, Cheeku and Tina are my best friends. – correct

Name : _______________________________

Section : _______________

Assessment Technique:

MCQ Based Worksheet

Home Work

Marks : 10   Time : 1 Day

1. **Directions: Read the sentences given below and tell which sentence has correct punctuation. Choose the answers from the options given below. (½ × 10 = 5 marks)**

1. (a) Where are you going?   (b) where are you going,
   (c) Where are you going.   (d) Where are you going !

2. (a) tomorrow is a holiday.   (b) Tomorrow is a holiday.
   (c) Tomorrow is a holiday?   (d) tomorrow is a Holiday !

3. (a) Mr. James is a painter by profession.
   (b) Mr. James is a painter by profession,
   (c) Mr. james is a painter by profession
   (d) Mr. james is a Painter by Profession.

4. (a) Tomorrow is earth day.   (b) Tomorrow is Earth Day.
   (c) Tomorrow is earth day   (d) Tomorrow is earth Day

5. (a) today is 15th January.   (b) Today is 15th january
   (c) today is 15th January   (d) Today is 15th January.

6. (a) cindrella is a fairytale story.   (b) Cinderella is a fairytale story.
   (c) Cinderella is a Fairytale story!   (d) Cinderella is a Fairytale story?

7. (a) Enid Blyton is a world famous story writer.
   (b) enid blyton is a world famous storssy writer.
   (c) Enid blyton is a world famous story writer.
   (d) enid Blyton is a world famous story writer.

8. (a) i was about nine years old said Rupa.
   (b) "i was about nine years old said rupa.
   (c) "I was about nine years old" said rupa.
   (d) "I was about nine years old", said Rupa.

9. (a) what will you write in your test.

   (b) what will you write in your test?

   (c) What will you write in your test!

   (d) What will you write in your test?

10. (a) India got independence on 15th August, 1947.

    (b) india got independence on 15th august 1947.

    (c) india got Independence on 15th august 1947.

    (d) India got independence on 15th August 1947!

II. Directions: Read the following passage carefully and fill in the blanks with the correct punctuation marks. Choose the answers from the options given below.

(½ × 10 = 5 marks)

Doing little work at home is good for children __(1)__ All the children should do some work at home __(2)__ Even if children do little work like, keeping their toys after playing __(3)__ it can be of great help to parents __(4)__ Children become responsible if they start doing little work at home __(5)__ It is important that children become responsible __(6)__ They can do little work like dress themselves and keep their clothes in place __(7)__ The children will love to help their parents with washing the cars __(8)__ going for grocery shopping or may be preparing their breakfast __(9)__ Helping your parents can be a daily exercise too __(10)__

1.	(a)	.	(b)	,	(c)	!	(d)	?
2.	(a)	.	(b)	,	(c)	!	(d)	?
3.	(a)	!	(b)	,	(c)	.	(d)	?
4.	(a)	.	(b)	,	(c)	!	(d)	?
5.	(a)	.	(b)	,	(c)	!	(d)	?
6.	(a)	.	(b)	,	(c)	!	(d)	?
7.	(a)	.	(b)	,	(c)	!	(d)	?
8.	(a)	.	(b)	,	(c)	!	(d)	?
9.	(a)	.	(b)	,	(c)	!	(d)	?
10.	(a)	.	(b)	,	(c)	!	(d)	?

CHAPTER 19

Articles

The words 'a' , 'an' and 'the' are called articles.

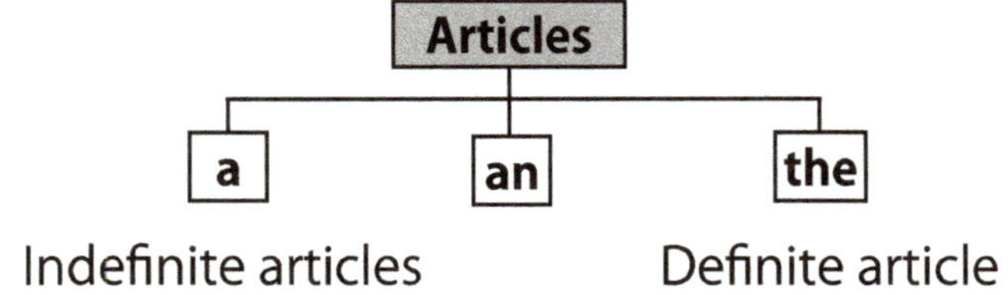

INDEFINITE ARTICLES

- The words **'a'** and **'an'** are indefinite articles.
- They are used with singular nouns.
- Use **'a'** before nouns that begin with a consonant.
- Use **'an'** before nouns that begin with a vowel. (a, e, i, o, u)

For example:
(a) Jai is reading a book.
(b) Would you like an apple?
(c) I have a dog and a cat.
(d) You will need a notebook and a pen.
(e) An elephant is a large animal.
(f) I need an umbrella.

DEFINITE ARTICLE

- The word **'the'** is called the definite article.
- Use **'the'** before a noun if you are talking about someone or something in particular.

For example :
(a) Daddy is sitting in **the** garden.
(b) **The** Taj Mahal is very beautiful.
(c) **The** Prime Minister of India is coming to our school today.
(d) I will wait for you in **the** car.
(e) **The** girls are playing.

Name : _______________________

Section : _____________

Assessment Technique:

Fillers

Class Work

Marks : 10   Time : 25 Minutes

I.   Directions : Choose the best answer and fill in the blanks.   **(1 × 4 = 4 marks)**

1.   _____________, _____________ and _____________ are called articles.

(a)   a, an, the   (b)   in, on, at   (c)   this, that, those.

2.   Articles are used before a _____________ or _____________ in a sentence.

(a)   noun, verb   (b)   noun, pronoun   (c)   noun, adjective

3.   Article 'the' is used when the thing mentioned is _____________.

(a)   a proper noun   (b)   a common noun   (c)   something special

4.   The article 'an' is used when the noun begins with a _____________.

(a)   vowel   (b)   consonant   (c)   alphabet

II.   Directions : Place an article before each picture given below.   **(1 × 6 = 6 marks)**

1. _______Strawberry   2. _______ Orange   3. _______Umbrella

4. _________ Clown   5. _________Earth   6. _________Indians

CHAPTER 20

Courtesy Words and Phrases

Courtesy means having a polite behaviour and good manners. It is very important to behave politely towards everyone. It makes us better human beings.

Let's learn about a few courtesy words and phrases

THANK YOU

We say thank you when:

- Someone gives us a gift or a compliment

- Someone does something for us

For example:

(a) "You look beautiful today."

  "Thank you."

(b) "Did you like your gift?"

  "Yes. Thank you."

(c) "Can you pass me that book?"

  "Yes."

  "Thank you."

We say **'please'** when we want someone to give us something or do something for us.

For example :

(a)   Can you lend me your pen, please?

(b)   Can you pass me that bag, please?

EXCUSE ME

We say excuse me when:

- We interrupt someone or ask someone to move.

- We sneeze loudly.

For example:

(a)   Excuse me, are you leaving?

(b)   Excuse me, may I borrow a pen?

I'M SORRY!

We say sorry when we make a mistake or do something wrong.

For example:

(a)   If you step on someone's foot, you will say – I'm sorry.

(b)   If you spill juice on your friend, you will say – I'm sorry.

Name : ___________________________

Section : ______________

Assessment Technique:

MCQ Based Worksheet

Home Work

Marks : 20 **Time : 1 Day**

I. **Directions : As children, we must know how to communicate with elders, strangers friends, in a sweet manner. Choose the option which you feel is correct.**

(1 × 10 = 10 marks)

1. Your uncle and aunt have come for dinner. You help your mother to serve. Your aunt thanks you. You reply :
   (a) It's okay.
   (b) Thank you !
   (c) It's my pleasure !

2. Your elder brother has joined Merchant Navy. He is going on his first trip abroad. You wish him :
   (a) All the best !
   (b) Bon voyage !
   (c) Good Bye !

3. An old friend meets you after several years. You say :
   (a) What a pleasant surprise !
   (b) Hello !
   (c) How are you !

4. You are unable to hear your teacher's instruction as you are sitting at the back of the class. You stand up and say :
   (a) I'm sorry.
   (b) I beg your pardon.
   (c) What ?

5. You have to give a speech in the class. The class is noisy. You say :
   (a) Shut up !
   (b) Quiet everyone!
   (c) May I have your attention, please!

6. It is New Year's Day. Your friend wishes you, "A Happy New Year." You say :
   (a) Happy New Year !
   (b) Same to you !
   (c) Welcome !

7. Your grandfather has come to visit you for a few days. As he is leaving, you may touch his feet and say :

(a) Goodbye grandfather !
(b) May you live long grandfather !
(c) Give me your blessings grandfather !

8. Your grandmother is not well. You visit her in the hospital. What will you say?
(a) Get well soon, granny !
(b) May God bless you, granny !
(c) All is well, granny !

9. If you are talking to someone and in between the conversation you sneeze, you say :
(a) Do not bother !
(b) Excuse me !
(c) Carry on with your conversation.

10. You dash into somebody, you say :
(a) Sorry !
(b) You must watch out when you walk!
(c) What are you up to?

II. Directions: Given below are certain real-life situations in the first column. The second column lists the various values of life. Match the situations with the values.

(1 × 10 = 10 marks)

Column A	Column B
1. You throw a chalk at your friend. It hits your teacher by mistake. You own up.	(i) Kindness
2. Your friend's sister has helped you in your Maths problems. You have scored well. You thank her.	(ii) Forgiving
3. A poor beggar boy comes to your doorstep. You give him a packet of biscuits.	(iii) Truthful
4. Your pet is hurt. You are in tears. You take him to the vet.	(iv) Helpful
5. An old man falls down while trying to cross the road. You help him up and take him home.	(v) Loving
6. Your friend quarrelled with you over homework. He says sorry the next day. You make up.	(vi) Grateful
7. Your sister is angry because she thinks you broke her vanity case. she is wrong. You are angry. But you do not display it.	(vii) Sympathetic
8. You are a good runner. You have faith that you will win the race.	(viii) Empathetic
9. A blindman wants to cross a busy road. You hold his hand and help him to cross.	(ix) Patience
10. Your best friend is unable to score good marks as his mother is ill. You understand his problem.	(x) Confident

CHAPTER 21

Prepositions

in, for, from, on, of, under,
by, at, with, over

Prepositions show a connection between other nouns and verbs. They tell us the position and place of the noun.

Most prepositions are little words such as – in, on, under, in front of, behind, over, through.

Let's learn more about prepositions and their uses

Preposition	Meaning	Example
In	Inside	1. Can we go in now? 2. My friend lives in Agra. 3. Milk is kept in the refrigerator.
On	To show that something is kept above another thing, and is touching it.	1. The food is kept on the table. 2. The cat jumped on me.
In front of	Ahead of something or someone	1. She was standing in front of me. 2. A bus came in front of our car.
Behind	At the back	1. She was sitting behind me. 2. He came from behind and scared me.
Under	Lower in position or height to something	1. We were sitting under a tree. 2. The cat is under the bed.
Over	1. Placed on the surface of somebody/something and covering it. 2. Above somebody/something	1. Some birds flew over our house. 2. She put a blanket over him.
Through	Going in from one side and coming out from the other side.	1. We came through the tunnel. 2. We went through the forest.

Name : _______________________

Section : _____________

Assessment Technique:

Fillers

Class Work

Marks : 10

Time : 20 Minutes

I. **Directions: Read the sentences given below and use prepositions given in the box to fill in the blanks.** **(½ × 10 = 5 marks)**

around, over, on, about, at, by, in, under, to, with, for, after, of

1. The cat is sitting _____________ the chair.

2. The ball is lying _____________ the table.

3. The purse is _____________ the handbag.

4. Garima had breakfast _____________ 9:00 A.M.

5. In Delhi people like to travel _____________ the metro.

6. Mahesh hit the ball _____________ the fence.

7. The students are sitting _____________ the teacher.

8. People are talking _____________ the incident.

9. All my friends are coming _____________ my birthday party tomorrow.

10. We are going to Chennai _____________ 25th of May.

II.   Directions: Read the sentences and fill in the blanks from the options given below

(½ × 10 = 5 marks)

1.   The little girl has been hiding ______ the table.

   (a) over   (b) under   (c) above   (d) on

2.   It is so hot, the sun is is almost ______ our heads.

   (a) above   (b) under   (c) in   (d) on

3.   Tim lay down ______ the grass.

   (a) in   (b) on   (c) above   (d) over

4.   I saw a rainbow ______ the sky.

   (a) in   (b) on   (c) over   (d) above

5.   Why are you so late? It's half _____seven.

   (a) past   (b) on   (c) at   (d) in

6.   My dad comes home _____six o' clock.

   (a) past   (b) at   (c) in   (d) on

7.   Always wash your hands ___soap before you start eating.

   (a) at   (b) in   (c) with   (d) on

8.   The bag is ___ the sofa.

   (a) above   (b) in   (c) on   (d) under

9.   Why are you hiding _____the chair?

   (a) over   (b) under   (c) behind   (d) on

10. Where is the ball? Is it _____the table?

   (a) above   (b) over   (c) on   (d) under

Name : _______________________

Section : _____________

Assessment Technique:

Check Box

Home Work

Marks : 20   **Time : 1 Day**

I.   Directions: In the picture given below, identify the prepositions and answer from the options given below. (1 × 4 = 4 marks)

1.   The girl is playing ____ the sand.
     (a) on   (b) in   (c) over   (d) above
2.   The boy is playing _____his dad.
     (a) on   (b) in   (c) with   (d) from
3.   The girl is making a castle ____her brother.
     (a) for   (b) over   (c) from   (d) under
4.   The boy is playing ____ the sea.
     (a) in   (b) with   (c) over   (d) from

II.   Directions : Read the sentences given below and recognize the prepositions. Choose the answers from the options given below. (1 × 6 = 6 marks)

1.   See, Rahul is sitting beside Ravi.
     (a) see   (b) Rahul   (c) sitting   (d) beside
2.   Reema's car has got stuck between the two trucks.
     (a) Reema   (b) car   (c) got   (d) between
3.   He is among one of the best guitar players.
     (a) he   (b) among   (c) best   (d) guitar
4.   When it came to choosing between a lie and a truth, he chose truth.
     (a) when   (b) came   (c) choosing   (d) between
5.   He walked across the lane.
     (a) he   (b) swalked   (c) across.   (d) lane
6.   Look! there is an old man standing on the roof of the building.
     (a) look   (b) there   (c) on   (d) standing

III. Directions: Read the passage and fill in the blanks from the options given below.

(1 × 10 = 10 marks)

The Thirsty Crow

Once upon a time there was a crow. It was very thirsty, so it was looking for water (1) ____ here and there. But it could not find water anywhere. It went (2)____ the mountains to look for water, but the mountains were dry. It was hot summer season! It went and sat(3) ____ top of the mountain to find water. (4)_____ there it saw a group of crocodiles playing (5)___ water (6) ____ a pond. The crow was so thirsty, that it wanted to quickly fly there and drink water. But it knew that it was very difficult to have water (7) ____ there. The crocodiles will not let it drink water (8) ____ that pond. So it thought of a plan. It flew away to that pond. "After it reached there, it said" I had a dream yesterday, I saw God. God has sent me here to tell you a few things but separately not together." This way the crow made the crocodiles fight (9) ________ each other. So, it sat (10) __________ the nearby tree and drank water when the crocodiles were busy fighting.

1. (a) of   (b) with   (c) from   (d) above

2. (a) between   (b) above   (c) on   (d) under

3. (a) in   (b) on   (c) with   (d) at

4. (a) from   (b) behind   (c) under   (d) below

5. (a) above   (b) at   (c) with   (d) on

6. (a) in   (b) on   (c) at   (d) from

7. (a) with   (b) from   (c) in   (d) on

8. (a) from   (b) above   (c) under   (d) between

9. (a) of   (b) with   (c) between   (d) at

10. (a) of   (b) in   (c) on   (d) over

Conjunctions

Conjunctions are words that are used to join two or more words or phrases.

Some common conjunctions are – **AND, BUT, OR**

Let's learn how to use each conjunction

AND

The conjunction '**and**' is used to link or join words that are similar to each other.

For example:

1. We ate rice **and** dal for lunch.

2. I like fruits **and** vegetables.

3. Radha's favourite subjects are Maths **and** English.

BUT

The conjunction '**but**' is used to join or link words that are different. They do not normally go together.

For example:

1. He writes quickly **but** neatly.

2. The weather was sunny **but** cold.

3. The kids were tired **but** happy.

OR

The conjunction '**or**' is used to give choices between two or more things.

For example:

1. You can have a sandwich **or** a burger.

2. We can go for a movie **or** stay at home.

3. Would you like noodles **or** soup?

Name : _______________________________

Section : _______________

Assessment Technique:

Fillers

Home Work

Marks : 20   Time : 1 Day

I.   Directions: Join sentences using appropriate conjunctions. Choose from the options provided.   **(1 × 10 = 10 marks)**

1.   Mr. Rajesh is very old _____________ he is physically fit   (and, or, but)

2.   Rahul _____________ Reema can run fast.   (and, or, but)

3.   Anand is rich _____________ greedy.   (and, or, but)

4.   The doctor treated the patient _________ he did not stop bleeding. (and, or, but)

5.   You must work hard ___________ you may not get good marks.   (but, and, or)

6.   The queen gave the beggars food ___________ clothes.   (and, or, but)

7.   We can eat Pizza ____________ burger.   (and, or, but)

8.   The hare ran ___________ the tortoise reached the finish line.   (and, or, but)

9.   Red, purple ____________ green are my favourite colours.   (and, or, but)

10. Turtles can swim ___________ walk.   (and, but, or)

II. Directions: After completing the activity, try and complete the following sentences.
                                                                                      (1 × 10 = 10 marks)

1.   You can study now **or**

2.   Raveena woke up early **and**

____

____

____

____

3. Ratika loves music **and**

____

____

4. The man caught the thief **but**

____

____

5. Sujata does not like sports **but**

____

____

6. Put on your shoes **and**

____

____

7. Megha is painting **and**

____

____

8. Ali works hard **but** Rohan

____

____

9. You must complete your work quickly **or**

____

____

10. I like bananas **and**

____

____

CHAPTER 23

Sequencing Sentences and Pictures

SENTENCE SEQUENCE

If sentences are not written in their correct order, they lose their meaning. In other words, we should write what comes first, followed by what comes second, and end with what comes at last.

Read the sentences given below.

- I wear my shoes.
- I put on my uniform.
- I brush my teeth.
- I wake up in the morning.
- I eat breakfast.
- I take a bath.

Do you think the order of these sentences is correct?

Now let's write these sentences in the correct order of activities.

- I wake up in the morning.
- I brush my teeth.
- I take a bath.
- I put on my uniform.
- I wear my shoes.
- I eat breakfast.

Now let's read a story.

My father gave me some seeds. I dug holes in the garden and planted those seeds. I watered the plants each day. I waited for a few weeks. After a few weeks, beautiful pink flowers began to grow.

Now arrange the sentences in the correct order.

- Some beautiful pink flowers began to grow.
- My father gave me seeds.
- I watered them each day.
- I planted the seeds.
- I dug holes in the garden.
- I waited for a few weeks.

The correct order

- My father gave me seeds.
- I dug holes in the garden.
- I planted the seeds.
- I watered them each day.
- I waited for a few weeks.
- Some beautiful pink flowers began to grow.

Let's learn how to sequence pictures in their correct order.

Making a Sandwich

1. In the first image we see two slices of bread, a knife and a bottle of jam.
2. In the second image, we see jam spread on the bread slice.
3. In the third image, we put the slices together.
4. In the fourth image, we take a bite of the sandwich.

Let's learn how to put these pictures in the correct order.

Going to School

In the correct order:

Waking up

Brushing teeth

Having bath

Combing hair

Eating breakfast

Going to school

Name : _______________________________

Section : _______________

Assessment Technique:

Sequencing the Picture

Home Work

Marks : 10

Time : 1 Day

I. **Directions: Complete the method by which Mala makes lemonade. Then sequence them in order** (½ × 10 = 5 marks)

ice cubes, water, glasses, lemonade, ice, lemon, fridge, spoon, sugar, little salt

(a) Mala takes out

_______________________ from the

_______________________.

(b) Mala stirs the jug of

____

with a

_______________________.

(c) Mala now squeezes a

____

in the jug of water. She also puts some

_______________________ and a

_______________ in it.

(d) Mala pours _______________ in the jug

to make _______________ .

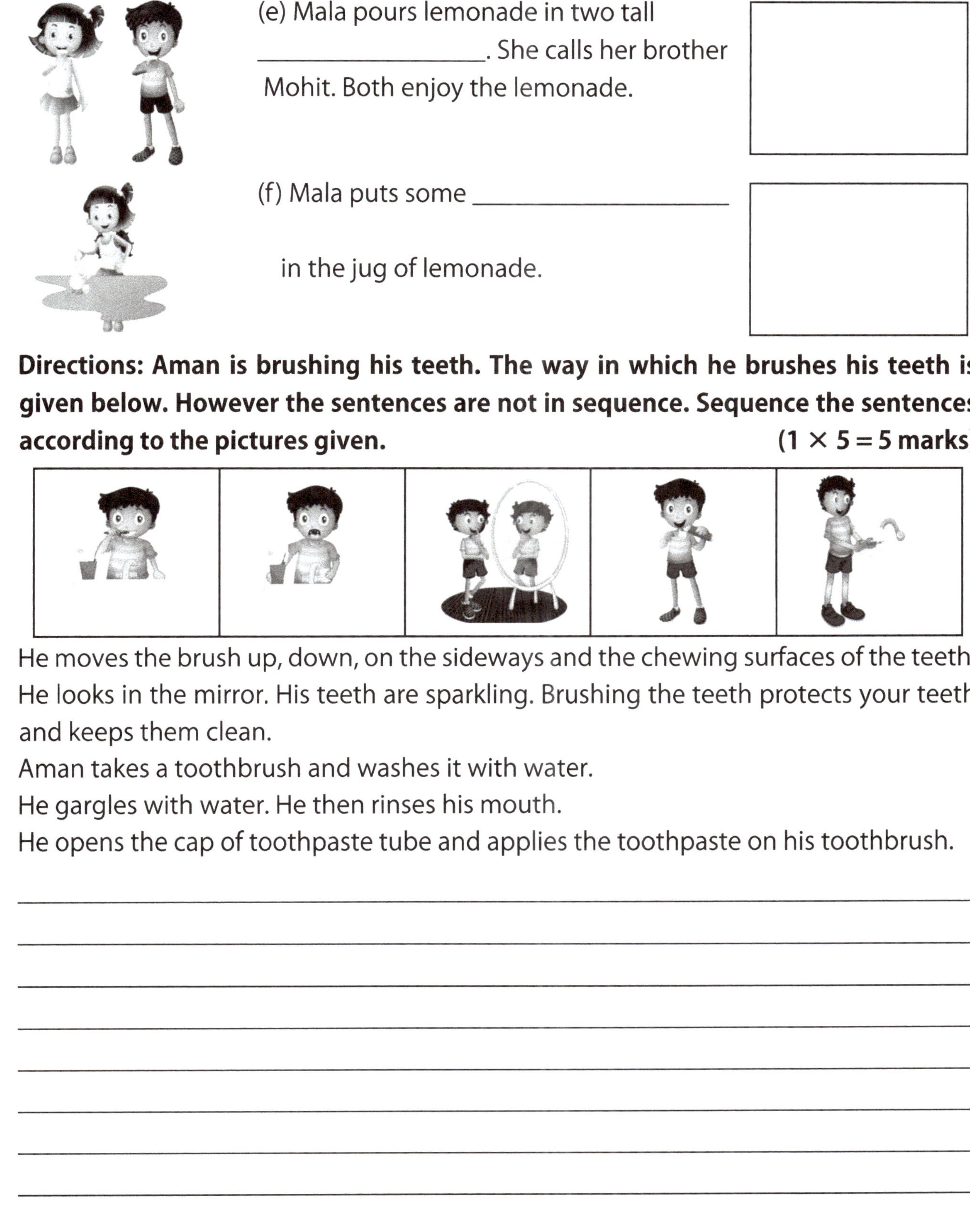

(e) Mala pours lemonade in two tall _________________. She calls her brother Mohit. Both enjoy the lemonade.

(f) Mala puts some _____________________ in the jug of lemonade.

II. Directions: Aman is brushing his teeth. The way in which he brushes his teeth is given below. However the sentences are not in sequence. Sequence the sentences according to the pictures given.   **(1 × 5 = 5 marks)**

1. He moves the brush up, down, on the sideways and the chewing surfaces of the teeth.
2. He looks in the mirror. His teeth are sparkling. Brushing the teeth protects your teeth and keeps them clean.
3. Aman takes a toothbrush and washes it with water.
4. He gargles with water. He then rinses his mouth.
5. He opens the cap of toothpaste tube and applies the toothpaste on his toothbrush.

1. ____

2. ____

3. ____

4. ____

5. ____

Name : _______________________

Section : ____________

Assessment Technique:

Picture Mystery

Home Work

Marks : 20   **Time : 1 Day**

Directions: Look at the pictures given below and arrange them in the proper sequence to form a story. Write a sentence for each of the pictures in the correct logical order. Also write the moral of the story. (Use separate sheet.)   **(2 × 10 = 20 marks)**

1.	2.	3.
fell into a dyer's pot	A jackal	went to jungle

4.	5.	6.
come out deep blue	called meeting of animals	called himself king of forest

7.	8.	9.
become very proud	blue jackal joined	is killed

10. 
a jackal howled

Describing a Picture

A picture can give us a lot of information about an event. Pictures can also tell us a story.

Tips for writing a good description of a picture.

1. Look at the picture carefully.
2. Note down the names of everything you see in the picture.
3. Now try to write down what you understood by seeing the picture.
4. Do not write more than five to six sentences.
5. You can either write about the event the picture is showing or make a story based on the picture.

Look at the picture given below and write a short description of the event. Use the hints given in the box.

Packing Trip Suitcase Mother Father Clothes Bag Cupboard Daughter Family

1. A family is packing their clothes.
2. Mother is taking out clothes from the cupboard
3. Daughter is putting clothes in a bag.
4. A suitcase is kept on the bed.
5. Father is helping to pack the clothes.
6. They are going for a trip.

See the picture given below. Now let's write a description with the help of the clues given in the box.

Trip Mumbai Aunt Cousins Luggage Suitcases Car Forgot Dog Timmy Clothes Toothbrush

My Aunt, my cousins and I are going on a trip in a car. We are going to Mumbai. We packed our suitcases a day before. We packed our clothes, shoes and toothbrushes in two suitcases. We tied the luggage to the top of the car. We packed everything but we forgot to take our dog Timmy. Timmy must be very sad.

Name : _______________________________

Assessment Technique:

Description Based

Section : ______________

Marks : 20

Time : 30 Minutes

I. **Directions: This is the picture of a cat called Fluffy. Using words from the box, write 5 lines about Fluffy. (Use separate sheet.)** (2 × 5 =10 marks)

white,	red ribbon,	brown eyes,	curly tail,	black spots

II. **Directions: Describe the pictures given below in one or two lines. (Use separate sheet.)** (2 × 5 = 10 marks)

1. ____

2. ____

3. ____

4. ____

5. ____

Name : ________________________

Section : ____________

Assessment Technique:

Application Based Worksheet

Marks : 10

Time : 30 Minutes

Directions: During the course of our daily activities, we come across many interesting incidents and enjoyable events. Analyse one such event/occasion you were a part of, in the format given below. (For example, a fair, a circus, a surprise party, etc.) (10 marks)

WHAT happened?	WHY did it happen?	WHERE did it happen

WHEN did it happen?	HOW did it happen?

Paragraph Writing

What is a paragraph?

A paragraph is made up of three to four sentences. Each sentence should have some meaning. All the sentences in a paragraph should be connected to one another.

For example:

Correct : I have a pet dog. Its name is Kara. It barks very loudly. I love my dog very much.

Incorrect : I have a pet dog. Shibu talks very loudly. We are going to eat dinner.

In the first example, the sentences are connected to one another. They are all about a dog Kara.

In the second example, the sentences are not connected to one another. They are about a dog, then Shibu and then it talks about dinner.

Let's learn how to write paragraphs using clues.

Clues: Mithu – parrot –green - talks – lives – cage – eats – fruits – favourite –guava

Paragraph: Mithu is a parrot. It is green in colour. It talks a lot. Mithu lives in a cage and eats fruits. Its favourite fruit is guava.

Clues: we – eat – vegetables – every day – healthy – love - eat– brinjal – lady finger – potato

Paragraph: We should eat vegetables everyday. They are healthy. I love to eat brinjals, lady finger and potatoes.

Name : ____________________

Section : ____________

Assessment Technique:

Application Based Worksheet

I. **Directions: Pick the words from the box and write a paragraph about your grandmother. (Use separate sheet.)** **(5 marks)**

sixty years old ________ goes for a walk ________ prays regularly ________ helps me with my homework ________ reads stories ________ loves me ________ cooks delicious food ________ grandmother is the best.

My Grandmother

II. **Directions: Write a paragraph of about 10 sentences about your favourite toy. Take the help of clues in the box. (Use separate sheet.)** **(5 marks)**

Name of the toy ________ type of toy (soft, metal) ________ Who gave it to you? ________ Why is it your favourite toy? ________ How do you keep the toy?

My Favourite Toy

Name : _______________________________

Section : _______________

Assessment Technique:

Application Based Worksheet

Class Work

Marks : 10   Time : 35 Minutes

I. Directions: (1 × 5 = 5 marks)

- Think of five sentences (facts) as soon as you hear the following words.
- Take 25-30 seconds to think.
- Write those sentences on the separate sheets.
- You may read those sentences to the class.

1. Bedtime stories (Clues - Fairy tales, Cindrella, Snowhite)
2. First day of school (Clues - how did you go?, who all did you meet?, did you make any friends?)
3. My favourite colour (Clues- name of the colour, why is it your favourite?, what all things you have are of that colour?)
4. Lunch time (Clues - things you like to eat, time at which you have lunch, who prepares your lunch?)
5. My birthday (Clues - date of birth, what do you do on your birthday?, whom do you celebrate it with?)

II. Directions :

If God grants you a wish and asks you to choose any superpower of your choice, which one will you choose? What will you do, once you get that superpower? **(Use separate sheet to write your answer.)** (1 × 5 = 5 marks)

You can create your own superpower or choose any of the following superpowers.

Ability to fly
Web sling
Heightened senses
Superhuman strength
Super speed
Best archer in the world
Mind control

SUPERMAN

SPIDERMAN

BATMAN

Name : _______________________

Section : _____________

Assessment Technique:

Creative Thinking

Marks : 10

Time : 1 Day

I. **Directions: What would happen if one morning everyone woke up and found out that the pets could talk? Write few lines from the point of view of a pet. You may take clues from the box given below. (Use separate sheet.)** **(5 marks)**

> Name of your pet - bumped with its leash or strap - started talking - talk about likes - e.g. bone - talk about dislikes - e.g. doesn't like to be trapped - stopped talking after few days.

II. **Directions : Your mother is very angry with your entire family. She feels that the family members are not following pleasant manners while eating. You have decided to help her by writing a paragraph describing in detail what it takes to be a respectful, pleasant person at dinner table. (Use separate sheet.)** **(5 marks)**

> Mother not happy - you write a paragraph - table manners - mention no talking, pray before eating, chew food properly, etc.

CHAPTER 26

Dialogue – Good Manners and Habits

It is important that we speak politely. Politeness is a sign of good manners.

Let's learn about good manners and habits with the help of dialogues.

GOOD MANNERS

1. Always say 'thank you' when someone gives you a gift or does something for you

2. Say 'please' when you want something from someone

3. Say 'sorry' if you hurt or disturb someone

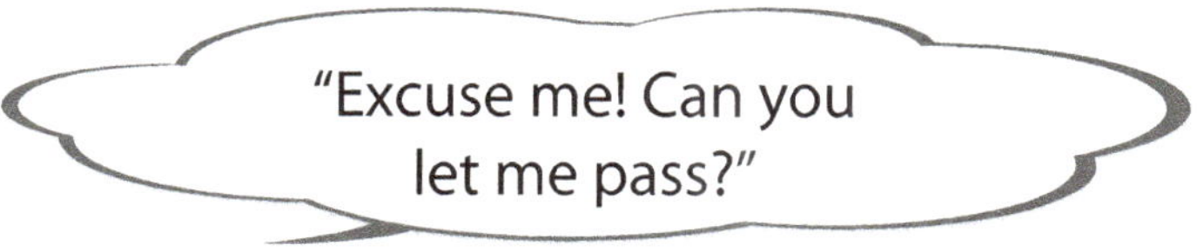

4. Say 'excuse me' if you are interrupting someone

GOOD HABITS

A habit is an activity that you do every day or regularly.

Good habit: A good habit is a habit that is healthy for your body.

For example: Brushing your teeth before going to sleep every night.

Here are a few more good habits.

1. Brushing your teeth twice everyday. Once in the morning and once at night.
2. Going to bed early at night.
3. Waking up early in the morning.
4. Eating healthy food such as vegetables, milk and fruits.
5. Taking a bath everyday
6. Combing your hair.
7. Speaking softly.
8. Throwing rubbish in the dustbin.
9. Helping your friends and family.
10. Doing your homework on time.

"I always go to sleep early at night and wake up early in the morning."
"You are a good boy."

"I don't feel good. I forgot to eat breakfast today."
"You should never skip breakfast. It is a bad habit."

Name : _________________________

Section : ____________

Assessment Technique:

Dialogue Completion

Home Work

Marks : 10   Time : 1 Day

I. **Directions: One dialogue is given to start the conversation between Mr. Rhino and Ms. Catty. Complete the further conversation between them in given dialogue boxes.**

(5 marks)

II. Directions: Three girls are talking with one another. Create a conversation and fill the dialogue boxes. One has been done for you. **(5 marks)**

1.

2.

3.

4.

5.

6.

Comprehension

Ram apple milkshake car go.

We are able to read these words given in the sentence above. We also know the meaning of each word written. But do we understand what is the meaning of this sentence? No. This sentence makes no sense. That is why we cannot understand what it means.

It is important to understand what we read.

Comprehension means understanding what one reads.

Let's read the passage given below and try to understand its meaning.

Shama does not like when it is very quiet. She is scared when there is no sound. She starts bouncing her ball. It makes a loud noise – Boing. Boing. Her father does not like when Shama is being noisy. So she stops playing with her ball. She covers her ears with her hands. Shama is surprised. She could hear so many different sounds. She could hear a bird chirping, a man walking on the street, a dog barking in the distance, a woman talking. She was no more bored. These sounds make her feel safe.

Now let's see how much we understood.

1. Fill in the blanks: Shama does not like when

   ____

2. When is Shama scared?
3. The ball bounced and made a loud noise of
   (a) Gong Gong   (b) Chirp Chirp
   (c) Ding-Dong   (d) Boing Boing
4. **Match the correct pairs:**
   (a) Bird   (i) talking
   (b) Man   (ii) barking
   (c) Dog   (iii) chirping
   (d) Woman   (iv) walking
5. **Word meaning.**
   1. Scared – to be in fear of something
   2. Quiet – when there is no sound
   3. Bouncing – moving up and down
   4. Surprised – being shocked
   5. Chirping – sound made by birds
   6. Barking – sound made by dogs

Name : _______________________

Assessment Technique:

Section : _____________

Retrieve the Facts

Class Work

Marks : 20   Time : 30 Minutes

I. **Directions: Read the following passage, then answer the questions below.**

The Taj Mahal is in Agra, India. It is about 200 kilometres east of Delhi, the capital of India. It is one of the most famous buildings in the world. It was built by Shah Jahan, one of the great Mughal emperors, in memory of his beautiful wife, Mumtaz Mahal, who died in 1631 AD. Shah Jahan loved his wife very much but she died when she was giving birth to her child. The emperor was heart broken and he decided to build a tomb for her so that people would always remember her name.

The construction work began in 1631 and was finished in 20 years. More than 20,000 workers and craftsmen helped to build the Taj Mahal which is made of white marble. It is surrounded by beautiful gardens. It is situated on the banks of river Yamuna.

1. **Write True or False.**   (½ × 5 = 2½ marks)

     (a)   The Taj Mahal was built by Shah Jahan. ____________________

     (b)   India is the capital of Delhi. __________________

     (c)   Mumtaz Mahal died in the year 1631. _______________

     (d)   20 thousands workers and craftsmen helped to build the Taj Mahal. ____________

     (e)   The Taj Mahal is one of the most famous buildings in the world. ____________

2. **Fill in the blanks:**   (½ × 5 = 2½ marks)

     (a)   Taj Mahal is in ____________________.

     (b)   Shah Jahan built it for his wife, __________________.

     (c)   It is made of __________________.

     (d)   It took ___________________ years to build the Taj Mahal.

     (e)   Taj Mahal is situated on the banks of __________________.

3. **Give the opposite of the following words:**   (½ × 4 = 2 marks)

     (a)   beautiful _____________   (b) remember _____________

     (c)   love _____________   (d) finish _____________

4. **Answer the following questions:**   (1 × 3 = 3 marks)

     (a)   How far is Taj Mahal from Delhi?

     ____

     ____

(b) How many workers and craftsmen were used to build the Taj Mahal?

____

____

(c) When and how did Mumtaz Mahal die?

____

____

II. Directions: Read the poem given below.

Autumn is the Time of Year

Autumn is the time of year
when changes start to happen here.
The days grow short. It's cold outside.
The birds fly south. The squirrels hide.
The leaves fall off of all the trees.
The garden pond begins to freeze.
Another summer's left behind.
It's winter soon, but I don't mind.
For autumn is the time when I
begin to dream of pumpkin pie.

1. **Answer the following questions:**   **(1 × 5 = 5 marks)**
   (a) Where do the birds fly?

   ____

   (b) Which animal hides?

   ____

   (c) What happens to the garden pond?

   ____

   (d) Which season comes before autumn?

   ____

   (e) Which season comes after autumn?

   ____

2. **Give the rhyming words of the following.**   **(½ × 6 = 3 marks)**

   a. year   ____________   d. behind ____________
   b. outside ____________   e. here   ____________
   c. trees   ____________   f. pie   ____________

3. **Fill in the blanks.**   **(½ × 4 = 2 marks)**

   a. The ____________ fall off the trees.   (leaves/fruits)
   b. The ____________ grow short.   (nights/days)
   c. The weather outside is ____________.   (hot/cold)
   d. The poet dreams of ____________.   (cakes/pies)

Name : _______________________

Section : ____________

Assessment Technique:

Picture Mystery

Class Work

Marks : 10

Time : 20 Minutes

Directions: Look at the picture of McSanta restaurant given below. Read carefully and then mark your answers. (1 × 10 = 10 marks)

1. What is the advertisement about?
    (a) Car repair shop
    (b) Restaurant
    (c) Household product shop
    (d) None of the above

2. What will yo do after entering McSanta?
    (a) Start playing
    (b) Sit on the chair and read the menu
    (c) Start eating from other's plate
    (d) Will do nothing

3. What is the name of the restaurant?
    (a) MC Anta
    (b) McSanta
    (c) Open
    (d) Santa Manta

4. How many products are there in the menu?
   (a)   5   (b)   11
   (c)   9   (d)   10
5. If any special offer is available, then what will you do?
   (a)   Avail the offer, straight away
   (b)   Ignore the offer
   (c)   Avail the offer, if it suits your need
   (d)   Ask to change the offer
6. What is the price of burger in the menu?
   (a)   ₹ 5   (b)   ₹ 10
   (c)   ₹ 20   (d)   It's for free
7. Cold drink is being given free with :
   (a)   Pizza   (b)   Burger
   (c)   Fingerchips   (d)   Sandwich
8. How many food items in the menu have cold drinks with them?
   (a)   3   (b)   8
   (c)   4   (d)   10
9. What is the price of the ice-cream?
   (a)   ₹ 10   (b)   ₹ 29.75
   (c)   ₹ 115   (d)   ₹ 35.40
10. Give another name to the restaurant.

   ____

Name : ________________________

Section : ____________

Assessment Technique:

Application Based Worksheet

Directions: Read the passage and answer the questions given below. Then mark your answers in the response grid. (1 × 10 = 10 marks)

It was a dark night. Suresh and his sister had come to the ice cream vendor. They wanted to buy ice-cream after dinner, for the whole family. The moon was out of sight. It was a no moon night. The children were feeling a little frightened. A dust storm was gathering in the horizon. The ice cream vendor was looking into his van box, searching for the twenty butter-scotch cones the children had ordered. All of a sudden, there was an explosive sound. All three of them ran for cover. The ice cream van toppled over. They thought it was a bomb explosion. A little later, Suresh peeped out of his hiding place. The ice cream vendor was coughing badly. His little sister Savita was crying. Suresh watched in wonder as a star-shaped spaceship landed in the park opposite to them.

There were multi-coloured lights on it. His companions too came out of their hiding place when they saw the expression on his face. An alien stepped out into the field. It looked all around. It waved a magic wand. The storm died down. Suresh was awestruck. His little sister clapped her hands. The ice cream vendor was smiling. The alien was so sensitive that it could hear and see it all. It vanished into the aircraft in a second. The ship took off. All three of them were too dazed to speak.

1. The timing of the story is in :

   (a) the past   (b) the present

   (c) the future   (d) not known

2. By setting of a story, we mean :

   (a) the message of the story

   (b) the time and place at which a story takes place

   (c) why was the story written?

   (d) what is the story about?

3. What season of the year is it?
    (a) Winter   (b) Autumn
    (c) Spring   (d) Summer
4. Tell us the time of the day :
    (a) Morning   (b) Afternoon
    (c) Night   (d) Evening
5. What is the story all about?
    (a) About life outside earth
    (b) About life
    (c) About nature
    (d) About people
6. Explain the meaning of the phrase "too dazed to speak"
    (a) Too shocked to speak
    (b) Not able to speak
    (c) Not able to move
    (d) Not able to see anything
7. Who is the main character of the story?
    (a) Suresh
    (b) Savita
    (c) The alien
    (d) Ice-cream vendor
8. How many members are there in Suresh's family?
    (a) 2   (b) 20
    (c) 22   (d) Not sure
9. Give a suitable title to the passage.

    ____

    ____

10. Give the antonyms of following words.
    (a) Dark = ____________________

    (b) Night = ____________________

1. Unscramble the given words.

   (a) kobo   (b) ysk   (c) kcol   (d) ousme

   (e) Bidlu   (f) wrog   (g) neov   (h) dogvo

2. Write the synonym of the words given below:

   (a) Little   (b) Quick   (c) Beautiful   (d) Big

   (e) Nice   (f) Brave   (g) Holy   (h) Fade

3. Give the five examples each of Countable Noun and Uncountable Noun.

4. Match the following

Column 'A'		Column 'B'
(a)	In a mosque	(i)	The Muslims kheel on the floor to pray
(b)	The Hindus pray	(ii)	You will find a cross
(c)	Sikhs go to the	(iii)	A church
(d)	On top of the most of churches	(iv)	In temples
(e)	Christian have mass in	(iv)	Gurudwara to worship

5. Write the plural words of the following.

   (a) Snake   (b) Box   (c) Knife   (d) Child

   (e) Monkey   (f) Window   (g) baby   (h) Horse

6. Write the opposite gender of the following

   (a) Son __________   (b) Lion __________

   (b) Bull __________   (d) Buck __________

   (e) Cock __________   (f) Nephew __________

   (g) Waiter __________   (h) Madam __________

7. Identify the people who do things for us and write their names.

(a) ___________________________

(b) ___________________________

(c) ___________________________

(d) ___________________________

(e) ___________________________

(f) ___________________________

(g) ___________________________

(h) ___________________________

8. Underline the pronoun(s) in each sentences.

(a) The ducks are so cute. They walk across the road every day.

(b) Tim bought a new car. He got a good deal.

(c) Marry went to school early. She is a great student.

(d) Sohan and Pintu work at the bakery. They love working there.

(e) Reema completed her homework. She is a great student.

9. Identify the Helping Verb and Action Verb in the following sentences. Circle the Helping Verb and Underline the fiction Verb.

(a) The boy is drawing in easy method.

(b) Did you jump in the pool?

(c) I was swimming in the lake.

(d) I can read Hindi words.

(e) Today. We might go to a movie.

(f) We were playing on the ground.

(g) I spoke to your friend.

(h) I will speak with your teacher.

10. Circle the word which rhymes with the given word.

(a) Well   =   sell   hen   tell

(b) One   =   bin   gun   won

(c) Kick   =   lick   pick   pain

(d) Jump   =   king   bump   lump

(e) King   =   sing   pick   wing

(f) By   =   win   buy   bye

11. Choose the correct opposite(s).

(a) Big   Small   Bad   Cry

(b) Happy   Smile   Sad   Big

(c) On   Up   Down   Under

(d) Man   Women   Men   Girl

(e)	Boy	Girl	Son	Boys
(f)	Up	Under	Down	Fly
(g)	Come	Some	Came	Go
(h)	Long	Thin	Short	Fat

12. Choose the correct conjunction.

(a) I bought cakes, candles ______________ ice-creams. (but/and)

(b) She is poor ___________ she is kind. (or/but)

(c) Do you prefer coffee____________ tea. (but/or)

(d) I love to eat pizza____________ burger. (and/but)

(e) Eagles fly alone, ____________ sheep flock together. (or/but)

(f) You must study, ____________ you will fail. (and/or)

13. Compound words are made from two words joined together, match them correctly.

(a)	basket	made
(b)	rail	road
(c)	school	cake
(d)	home	port
(e)	pass	boat
(f)	water	ball
(g)	cup	house
(h)	tug	proof

14. Complete the given sentence with suitable preposition **behind** or **near** or **inside**. Refer to the pictures to fill in the blanks.

(a) The flower is ___________ the watering can.

(b) The frog is ___________ the jar.

(c) The jar is ___________ a small stone.

(d)   I have a car. It is ___________ the big truck.

(e)   I can see a pole __________ the truck and my car.

(f)   Kunal goes for morning walk daily. His dog walks __________ him.

(g)   Kunal is __________ a tea stall.

15. Circle the correct article that goes before each word.

(a)   A   An   The   Starfish

(b)   A   An   The   Books

(c)   A   An   The   Spider

(d)   A   An   The   Moon

(e)   A   An   The   Duck

(f)   A   An   The   Shoes

(g)   A   An   The   Pencil

(h)   A   An   The   Egg

SOLUTIONS

Chapter-1 Sentences

Application Based Worksheet-01

I.
1. Subject: I
   Predicate: want a new car
2. Subject: Rajiv
   Predicate: is nice
3. Subject: The sun
   Predicate: is moving
4. Subject: Kavita
   Predicate: wrote the letter
5. Subject: The letter
   Predicate: was written by Namita
6. Subject: The farmers
   Predicate: are ploughing the field
7. Subject: Sachin Tendulkar
   Predicate: is an amazing player
8. Subject: The storm clouds
   Predicate: are getting darker
9. Subject: Dogs, cats and rabbits
   Predicate: make the best pets
10. Subject: All people of the town
    Predicate: ran away from the burning building

II.
1. watered the flowers
2. flew the air plane
3. barked all night long
4. cut the boy's hair
5. blew in the wind

III.
1. A buzzing bee
2. An eye doctor
3. The house plant
4. A grey dolphin
5. A big spider

Fillers Worksheet-02

I.
1. D
2. I
3. D
4. I
5. D
6. D
7. I
8. I
9. D
10. D

II.
2. How is the little baby?
3. Are you taking your medicines?
4. Who gave you these chocolates?
5. Where does your grandmother live?
6. Who won the all rounder award this year?
7. What do you like to play? / What are your hobbies?
8. Which ball do you like?
9. Why didn't you come to my birthday party?
10. How did you get hurt?

1. Today I am feeling very happy.
2. Birds are flying in the sky.
3. Radhika is a good student.
4. Sreeram is always fighting with his sister.
5. Watching T.V. for a long time is injurious to health.
6. Children love to eat fast food.
7. We must pray at least once every day.
8. I have a dog in my house.
9. We must exercise daily.
10. There is a broken chair in the lobby.

Jumble Fumble Worksheet-04

I.
1. Stars shine in the sky.
2. Cow gives us milk.
3. I have an elder brother.
4. My sister is very naughty.
5. Kites fly in the sky.
6. There are trees on the hill.
7. Should we protect trees?
8. The gardener waters plants.
9. Where do you want to go?
10. Do you like this book?

II.
1. knife
2. tyre
3. lock
4. chain
5. oven
6. eight
7. horse
8. tables
9. rainbow
10. mouse

Chapter-2 Synonyms, Homonyms and Homophones

MCQ Based Worksheet-05

I.
1. (b) make
2. (c) fearless
3. (a) develop
4. (c) fix
5. (b) clever
6. (c) dim
7. (a) rubbish
8. (b) godly

II.
1. Suresh always keeps his bedroom **neat**.
2. The monkey **leapt** off the tree trunk.
3. Mahesh likes to live in a **large** house.
4. The landlord **shouted** at the boys for plucking the mangoes.
5. Everyone started laughing when the **joker** walked in.
6. Rupa is a **wonderful** girl.

I. 1. cross 2. ruler 3. left 4. break 5. ruler
6. left 7. break 8. cross 9. table 10. free

II. 1. (a) hare 2. (b) I 3. (b) days
4. (b) very 5. (a) right

Chapter-3 Naming Words

Picture Based Worksheet-07

I. 1. proper 2. common 3. common 4. proper 5. proper

II. 1. P 2. C 3. P 4. C 5. P
6. P 7. C 8. C 9. P 10. C

Picture Based Worksheet-08

I. 1. U 2. U 3. C 4. U 5. U
6. C 7. U 8. C 9. U 10. U

II.

Countable Nouns	Uncountable Nouns
cat	ketchup
clock	rice
pineapple	honey
onions	tea
pens	flour

Picture Based Worksheet-09

I. 1. Gandhi Jayanti

2. Republic Day

3. Independence Day

II. 1. Diwali 2. Holi 3. Christmas 4. Dusshera 5. Baisakhi
6. Raksha Bandhan
7. Janmasthami

I. 1. sea- saw   2. round about   3. Jungle Gym

    4. slide   5. swing

II. **Answers may vary.**

Chapter-4 Accessories

Picture Based Worksheet-11

I. **Wardrobe of Mehul**

    1. Shirt   2. Cufflinks   3. Shoes

    4. Trousers   5. Socks   6. Tie

    7. Watch   8. Belt   9. Hat and cap

    10. Wallet

    Wardrobe of Reena

    1. Frock   2. Skirt   3. Sandals

    4. Bangles   5. Earrings   6. Scarf

    7. Handbag   8. Necklace   9. Hair clips

    10. Hat

Chapter-5 Food

Picture Based Worksheet-12

MENU CARD

Cheese Light

Deluxe Non–Veg

Simple Veg.

Veg. King size

Names of missing ingredients:

burger buns, onions, tomatoes, lettuce, cheese, tomato ketchup

Create your own burgers: Do it yourself.

Match Attach Worksheet-13

I.

	Column A		Column B
1.	Sikhs go to the	(iv)	Gurudwara to worship
2.	Christians have mass in	(iii)	a Church
3.	In a Mosque	(i)	the Muslims kneel on the floor to pray
4.	On top of most of the churches	(ii)	you will find a cross
5.	The Hindus pray	(v)	in temples

II.

1.	BUDDHISM	2.	HINDUISM
3.	CHRISTIANITY	4.	ISLAM
5.	JAINISM	6.	QURAN
7.	GEETA	8.	BIBLE
9.	GURU GRANTH SAHIB	10.	JUDAISM

Chapter-7 One and Many

Transform Sentences Worksheet-14

I.

2. The girls are dancing on the stage.

3. The tigers were chasing the deers.

4. The children love to eat ice creams.

5. There are beautiful roses in my garden.

II.

1. (b) Thieves

2. (a) Wolves

3. (b) Knives

4. (b) Monkeys

5. (a) Babies

Chapter-8 Masculine and Feminine

Gender Conversion Worksheet-15

I. 1. daughter   2. sir   3. peahen   4. priestess   5. washerwoman
6. bridegroom   7. queen   8. mare   9. headmistress   10. poetess

II.
1. My **sister** is good at studies.
2. Vishnu's **grandmother** tells him stories at bed time.
3. The **waitress** was very polite.
4. His **niece** is a famous artist.
5. Reshma's **mother** is a manager in a bank.
6. My **uncle** bought me a beautiful leather jacket.
7. The **tigress** attacked the animals.
8. The **actress** is also a good singer.
9. The **princess** went hunting in the jungle.
10. The **heroine** was riding on a motorcycle.

Chapter-9 One Word Substitution

Crossword Worksheet-16

I.

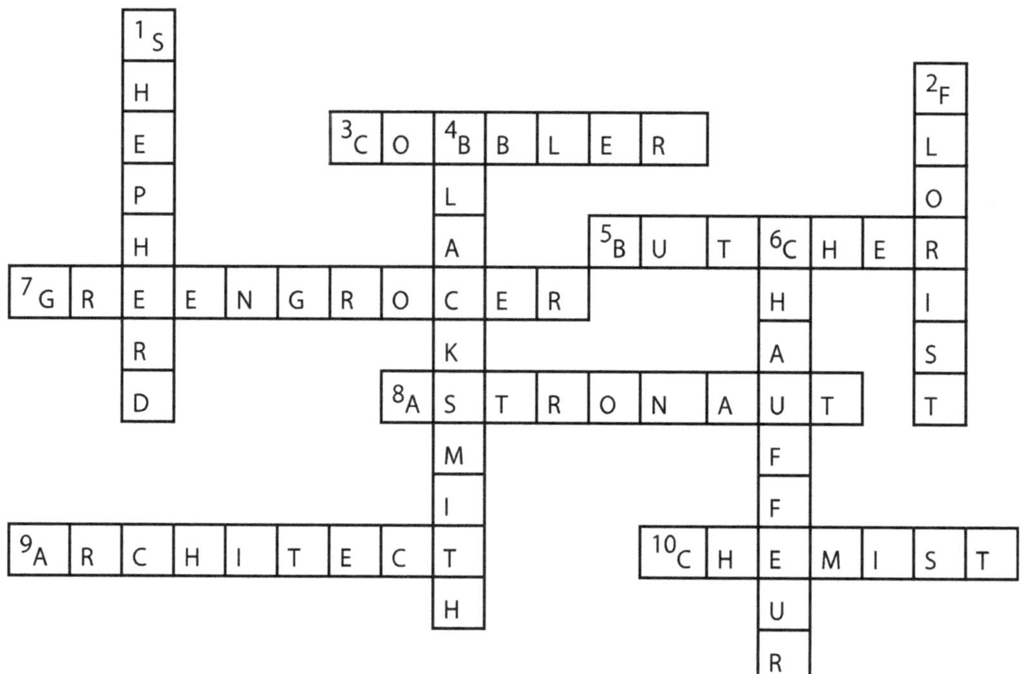

II.	**Column A**	**Column B**
	1. A place were aeroplanes are kept.	(viii) hanger
	2. A bunch of flowers.	(ix) bouquet
	3. A group of fish.	(x) school
	4. A book containing words and their meanings.	(vii) dictionary
	5. Feminine of wizard.	(i) witch
	6. A room where you will find lots of books.	(ii) library
	7. A place to keep clothes.	(iii) wardrobe
	8. A group of dancers.	(iv) troupe
	9. A group of musicians.	(v) orchestra
	10. A group of bees.	(vi) swarm

Chapter-10 Pronouns

Application Based Worksheet-17

I. **Answers may vary.**

1. his	2. they	3. her	4. my, my/his, their
5. He	6. She, they	7. we	8. He
9. his, his	10. you, I		

II. 1. **It** was summer vacation. Suresh was feeling very bored. **He** decided to play in the garden. Even as **he** was throwing the ball towards the wall, **he** heard a loud thud. The thud was followed by a shout. **He** looked upwards. A lady was looking out of a broken window. **She** was looking very angry. The old windowpanes were broken. **It** was a sorry sight. Suresh was so frightened that **he** ran away. The angry lady was waving **her** hands. The broken part of the window fell on **her** head. **She** fell back in fright.

Fillers Worksheet-18

I.

1. he	2. they	3. it	4. me	5. you
6. she	7. her	8. it	9. I	10. us

II.

1. his, it	2. she, her	3. them	4. he, her	5. They
6. They	7. We			

Chapter-11 Action Words

MCQ Based Worksheet-19

I.

1. (b) rises	2. (b) loves
3. (a) ran	4. (a) read
5. (c) fighting	6. (b) went
7. (b) leapt	8. (b) drew
9. (b) blew	10. (b) Did
11. (c) fallen	12. (c) forgotten

II. 1. (a) dancing   2. (c) shattered
     3. (a) walking   4. (b) spread
     5. (b) swaying   6. (c) celebrated
     7. (c) riding   8. (a) doing

Chapter-12 Helping Verbs

MCQ Based Worksheet-20

1. (b) was   2. (d) is/was   3. (b) were
4. (d) am/was   5. (b) was   6. (d) has/had
7. (d) has/had   8. (c) have   9. (b) have
10. (c) had

Fillers Worksheet-21

1. has   2. have   3. has   4. has   5. has
6. have   7. has   8. have   9. have   10. has

Chapter-13 Rhyming Words

Choose and Colour Worksheet-22

I.   1. sight, bright   2. class, grass
     3. coat, boat   4. puddle, double
     5. dome, foam   6. toon, moon
     7. mouse, louse   8. bed, bread
     9. hop, crop   10. rest, nest

II.   **Column A**   **Column B**
     1. owl   (vii)   growl
     2. cow   (viiii) now
     3. bull   (ix)   pull
     4. yellow   (x)   fellow
     5. book   (i)   shook
     6. mist   (ii)   fist
     7. ship   (iii)   hip
     8. foot   (iv)   put
     9. band   (v)   sand
     10. gate   (vi)   late

Chapter-14 Describing Words and Comparison of Adjectives

Identification Based Worksheet-23

I.
1. Noun : trip, Disneyland — Adjective: exciting
2. Noun : children, cartoons — Adjective: interesting
3. Noun : magician, hankies, hat — Adjective: famous, colourful
4. Noun : Ravish, wrestlers, WWF — Adjective: powerful
5. Noun : vase, flowers — Adjective: expensive, colourful, beautiful
6. Noun : Radhika, cupboard, toys — Adjective: little, electronic
7. Noun : boy, milk — Adjective: careless, hot
8. Noun : grandmother, house, garden — Adjective: big, beautiful
9. Noun : giant, boy — Adjective: huge, little
10. Noun : spaceship, park — Adjective: giant, lonely

II. Answers may vary

1. honest, patriotic		2. large, deep	
3. yummy, cheap		4. amusing, joyful	
5. hardworking, enthusiastic		6. cute, beautiful	
7. amazing, white		8. highest, snowy	
9. exciting, thrilling		10. helpful, kind	

Degree Comparisons Based Worksheet-24

1. Comparative: cleaner — Superlative: cleanest
2. Comparative: taller — Superlative: tallest
3. Comparative: slower — Superlative: slowest
4. Comparative: heavier — Superlative: heaviest
5. Comparative: more cheerful — Superlative: most cheerful
6. Comparative: less — Superlative: least
7. Comparative: older — Superlative: oldest
8. Comparative: more beautiful — Superlative: most beautiful
9. Comparative: more difficult — Superlative: most difficult
10. Comparative: whiter — Superlative: whitest

Chapter-15 Opposites

Reverse Converse Worksheet-25

I.

1. right	2. many	3. new	4. early	5. over
6. smallest	7. never	8. easy	9. dirty	10. push

II.

1. sick	2. tall	3. difficult	4. foolish	5. cold
6. fat	7. empty	8. right	9. asleep	10. tidy

Fillers Worksheet-26

I.
1. (a) This
2. (b) These
3. (c) that
4. (a) Those
5. (b) These
6. (a) Those
7. (e) that
8. (b) This
9. (b) that
10. (c) These

II.
1. those
2. those
3. these
4. That
5. these
6. that
7. This
8. those
9. these
10. them

Chapter-17 Compound Words

Fillers Worksheet-27

I.
1. starfish
2. wallpaper
3. rattlesnake
4. spaceship
5. scarecrow
6. supernatural
7. thanksgiving
8. flashlight
9. wildlife
10. mailbox

1. flashlight
2. thanksgiving
3. starfish
4. wallpaper
5. rattlesnake
6. spaceship
7. scarecrow
8. wildlife
9. supernatural
10. mailbox

II.

	Column A		Column B		
2.	horse	(viii)	cart	(b)	horse-cart
3.	super	(xi)	man	(c)	superman
4.	black	(iii)	board	(d)	blackboard
5.	ink	(vii)	pot	(e)	ink pot

6.	railway	(ix)	station	(f)	railway station
7.	sun	(v)	light	(g)	sunlight
8.	rain	(x)	bow	(h)	rainbow
9.	bed	(vi)	sheet	(i)	bedsheet
10.	ice	(iv)	cream	(j)	ice cream
11.	grass	(ii)	hopper	(k)	grasshopper

Chapter-18 Punctuation Marks

MCQ Based Worksheet-28

I.
1. (a) Where are you going?
2. (b) Tomorrow is a holiday.
3. (a) Mr. James is a painter by profession.
4. (b) Tomorrow is Earth Day.
5. (d) Today is 15th January.
6. (b) Cinderella is a fairytale story.
7. (a) Enid Blyton is a world famous story writer.
8. (d) "I was about nine years old", said Rupa.
9. (d) What will you write in your test?
10. (a) India got independence on 15th August 1947.

II. (.) full stop, (,) comma, (!) exclamation marks, (?) question mark

| 1. (a) . | 2. (a) . | 3. (b) , | 4. (a) . | 5. (a) . |
| 6. (a) . | 7. (a) . | 8. (b) , | 9. (a) . | 10. (a) . |

Chapter-19 Articles

Fillers Worksheet-29

I.
1. (a) a, an, the
2. (c) noun, adjective
3. (c) something special
4. (a) vowel

II.

| 1. A | 2. An | 3. An | 4. A | 5. The |
| 6. The | | | | |

MCQ Based Worksheet-30

I. **Answers may vary.**

1. (c) It's my pleasure!
2. (a) All the best!
3. (a) What a pleasant surprise!
4. (b) I beg your pardon.
5. (c) May I have your attention, please!
6. (b) Same to you!
7. (c) Give me your blessings grandfather!
8. (a) Get well soon, granny!
9. (b) Excuse me!
10. (a) Sorry!

II.

	Column A		Column B
1.	You throw a chalk at your friend. It hits your teacher by mistake. You own up.	(iii)	Truthful
2.	Your friend's sister has helped you in your Maths problems. You have scored well. you thank her.	(vi)	Grateful
3.	A poor beggar boy comes to your doorstep. You give him a packet of biscuits.	(i)	Kindness
4.	Your pet is hurt. You are in tears. You take him to the vet.	(v)	Loving
5.	An old man falls down while trying to cross the road. You help him up and take him home.	(iv)	Helpful
6.	Your friend quarrelled with you over homework. He says sorry the next day. You make up.	(ii)	Forgiving
7.	Your sister is angry because she thinks you broke her vanity case. She is wrong. You are angry. But you do not display it.	(ix)	Patience
8.	You are a good runner. You have faith that you will win the race.	(x)	Confident
9.	A blindman wants to cross a busy road. You hold his hand and help him to cross.	(vii)	Sympathetic
10.	Your best friend is unable to score good marks as his mother is ill. You understand his problem.	(viii)	Empathetic

Chapter-21 Prepositions

Fillers Worksheet-31

I. 1. on/under 2. under/on 3. in 4. at 5. by
6. over 7. around 8. about 9. for 10. on

II. 1. (b) under 2. (a) above
3. (b) on 4. (a) in
5. (a) past 6. (b) at
7. (c) with 8. (c) on
9. (c) behind 10. (d) under

Check Box Worksheet-32

I. 1. (b) in   2. (c) with
    3. (a) for   4. (b) in

II. 1. (d) beside   2. (d) between
    3. (b) among   4. (d) between
    5. (c) across   6. (c) on

III. 1. (c) from   2. (b) above
    3. (b) on   4. (a) From
    5. (c) with   6. (a) in
    7. (b) from   8. (a) from
    9. (d) with   10. (c) on

Chapter-22 Conjunctions

Fillers Worksheet-33

I. 1. but   2. and   3. but   4. but   5. or
    6. and   7. and, or   8. but   9. and   10. and

II. Answers may vary.

1. you can take rest.   2. had tea.
3. dance.   4. he ran away
5. she likes reading.   6. get ready.
7. Reema is cooking   8. is lazy.
9. you might miss the game.   10. apples.

Chapter-23 Sequencing Sentences and Pictures

Sequencing the Picture Worksheet-34

I. (a) ice, fridge

(b) lemonade, spoon

(c) lemon, sugar, little salt

(d) water, lemonade

(e) glasses

(f) ice – cubes

(a) 3	(b) 5	(c) 2	(d) 1	(e) 6	(f) 4

II. 1. Aman takes a toothbrush and washes it with water.

2. He opens the cap of the toothpaste tube and applies the toothpaste on his toothbrush.

3. He makes the brush wet again and rubs the brush on the teeth. He moves the brush up, down, on the sideways and inside his mouth too.

4. He gargles his mouth with water. He then rinses his mouth.

5. He looks in the mirror. His teeth are sparkling. Brushing the teeth protects your teeth and keeps them clean.

Picture Mystery Worksheet-35

1. The jackal fell into the dyer's pot. (2)
2. A jackal went into a village. (1)
3. He went back into the jungle. (4)
4. He came out deep blue in colour. (3)
5. He called the meeting of animals. (5)
6. He called himself the king of forest. (6)
7. He became very proud. (7)
8. The blue jackal joined. (9)
9. The blue jackal is killed. (10)
10 A jackal howled. (8)

Chapter-24 Describing a Picture

Description Based Worksheet-36

I. Answers may vary.

II. Answers may vary.

Application Based Worksheet-37

Answers may vary.

Chapter-25 Paragraph Writing

Application Based Worksheet-38

I. Answers may vary.

My grandmother is sixty years old. Her name is Vidya Srivastava. She goes for a walk every evening. She prays regularly in the morning. She helps me with my homework too. She reads interesting stories to me. She loves me a lot. She cooks delicious food. My grandmother is the best.

II. Answers may vary.

I. Answers may vary.

II. Answers may vary.

Creative Thinking Worksheet-40

I. Answers may vary.

II. Answers may vary.

Table Manners

Table manners are the rules we should keep in mind while eating. This also includes using utensils for eating. Few table manners we should keep in mind are:

We should wash our hands before eating.

We should say our prayers before eating.

We should eat with our mouth closed. We should not talk while eating.

We should not make noise while eating.

We should not waste food.

Chapter-26 Dialogue – Good Manners and Habits

Dialogue Completion Worksheet-41

I. Answers may vary.

Rhino: Hi! Catty. How are you? Why are you looking so shocked?

Catty: Sir, I have lost my bag which contained important documents.

Rhino: Please describe the bag.

Catty: It was a brown coloured bag with golden strap. The documents contained information about good manners and habits.

Rhino: I will help you. Let me call the officer in-charge.

Catty: Thank you sir.

II. Answers may vary.

Chapter-27 Comprehension

Retrieve the Facts Worksheet-42

I. 1. (a) True
   (b) False
   (c) True
   (d) True
   (e) True

II. 1. (a) The birds fly south
   (b) Squirrels hide
   (c) The garden pond begins to freeze
   (d) Summer season
   (e) Winter season

2. (a) Agra
    (b) Mumtaz Mahal
    (c) White Marble
    (d) 20 years
    (e) river Yamuna
3. (a) ugly
    (b) forget
    (c) hate
    (d) begin

2. (a) here
    (b) hide
    (c) freeze
    (d) mind
    (e) year
    (f) I
3. (a) leaves
    (b) days
    (c) cold
    (d) pies

4. (a) Taj Mahal is 200 kilometers east of Delhi.
    (b) 20 thousand workers were used to build the Taj Mahal.
    (c) Mumtaz Mahal died in 1631 A.D. while giving birth to her child.

Picture Mystery Worksheet-43

1. (b) Restaurant
2. (b) Sit on the chair and read the menu
3. (b) McSanta
4. (d) 10
5. (c) Avail the offer, if it suits your need
6. (b) 10 ₹
7. (a) Pizza
8. (c) 4
9. (b) 29.75
10. King Santa **(Answers may vary.)**

Application Based Worksheet-44

I. 1. (a) The past
    2. (b) The time and the place at which a story takes place
    3. (d) Summer
    4. (c) Night
    5. (a) About life outside earth
    6. (a) Too shocked to speak
    7. (c) The alien
    8. (b) 20
    9. The Outer World (Answers will vary)
    10. (a) Light   (b) Day

COMBINED PRACTICE SOLUTIONS

1. (a) Book
    (b) Sky
    (c) Lock
    (d) Mouse
    (e) Build
    (f) Grow
    (g) Oven
    (h) Good

2. (a) small
    (b) Fast
    (c) Pretty
    (d) Large
    (e) kind
    (f) Fearless
    (g) Pure
    (h) dim

3. **Countable noun**
    (a) Apple
    (b) Chair
    (c) Bottle
    (d) Table
    (e) Bag

    Uncountable noun
    (a) Rice
    (b) Sugar
    (c) water
    (d) Butter
    (e) gas

4. (a) (i)
    (c) (v)
    (e) (iii)
    (b) (iv)
    (d) (ii)

5. (a) Snakes
    (b) Boxes
    (c) Knives
    (d) Children
    (e) Monkeys
    (f) Windows
    (g) babies
    (h) Horses

6. (a) Daughter
    (b) Lioness
    (c) Cow
    (d) Doe
    (e) Hen
    (f) Niece
    (g) Waitress
    (h) Sir

7. (a) Teacher
    (b) Doctor
    (c) Potter
    (d) Policeman
    (e) Fireman
    (f) Cook
    (g) shopkeeper
    (h) Driver

8. (a) The ducks are so cute. They walk across the road every day.
    (b) Tim bought a new car. He got a good deal.
    (c) Mary went to school early. She is a great student.
    (d) Sohan and pintu work at the bakery. They love working there.
    (e) Reema completed her homework. She is a great student.

9. (a) The boy (is) drawing in easy method.
    (b) (Did) you jump in the pool?
    (c) I (was) swimming in the lake.
    (d) I (can) read Hindi words.
    (e) Today, We (might) go to a movie.

(f) We (were) playing on the ground.

(g) I <u>spoke</u> to your friend.

(h) I (will) speak with your teacher.

10. (a) well   =   sell, tell

    (b) one   =   gun, won

    (c) kick   =   lick, pick

    (d) jump   =   bump, lump

    (e) King   =   sing, wing

    (f) By   =   buy, bye

11. (a) Small   (b) Sad

    (c) Under   (d) Women

    (e) Girl   (f) Down

    (g) Go   (h) Short

12. (a) And

    (b) but

    (c) or

    (d) and

    (e) but

    (f) or

13. (a) basket   made

    (b) rail   road

    (c) school   cake

    (d) home   port

    (e) pass   boat

    (f) water   ball

    (g) cup   house

    (h) tug   proof

14. (a) Behind

    (b) inside

    (c) near

    (d) Behind

    (e) between

    (f) behind

    (g) near

15. (a) A   (b) The

    (c) A   (d) The

    (e) A   (f) The

    (g) A   (h) An